I am moving to Sweden!

Everything you need for your
NEW
Swedish life

Mirjam Taylor

Copyright© 2021 Mirjam Taylor
(Taylor Literary Creations)

First edition:

I'm moving to Sweden! - Everything you need for your new Swedish life. All rights reserved. No part of this publication may be reproduced, stored in a retrieval system or transmitted in any form or by any means electronic, mechanical, photocopying recording or otherwise without the prior written permission of the author.

Table of Contents

Acknowledgements 1
Foreword 2
   So, you're moving to Sweden! 2
   Key facts about Sweden 3
   A mini dictionary for this book 3
Studying in Sweden 6
   Why study in Sweden? 6
      What can I do on a student visa? 7
   Who can study in Sweden? 8
      Getting a bachelor degree 9
      Getting a master degree 9
      Getting a Ph.D. 10
   How to study in Sweden? 10
      Becoming an exchange student 10
      Studying as an adult 12
      Becoming a language student 14
   Getting your student visa 17
      EU/EEA countries and Nordic countries 18
      Non-EU/EEA countries 18

   Summary 21
Working in Sweden 24
   Why work in Sweden? 24
      1. Globalization 24
      2. Innovation 25
      3. Sustainability 25
      4. Equality 26
      5. Balanced life 26

A one-year working holiday 28
  Who can apply for the working holiday program? 29
  Requirements for a working holiday residence permit 30

Company transfers 31
  Who can apply for an ICT permit? 32
  Requirements for an ICT permit 32

Independently looking for work 34
  Residents of EU/EEA countries 34
  Residents of non-EU/EEA countries 35

Digital nomad/remote work 36
  Applying for a job 36

Getting your work visa 37
  Getting your working holiday residence permit 37
  Getting your ICT permit 38
  Getting your "independent" work and resident permit 40
  Getting your au pair work permit 41

Summary 43

Religious activities in Sweden 46

Religion in Sweden 46

Getting your religious activities visa 47
  Getting your visa to visit Sweden for religious purposes 48
  Getting your visitor's permit for religious purposes 50

Summary 52

Volunteering or being a trainee in Sweden 54

The European Solidarity Corps 54

Getting your volunteering visa 56
  Residence permit for volunteers 56
  Visa for volunteer work or an internship 58
  Visitor's permit for a volunteer or trainee 59
  Work permit for traineeship through international exchange 61
  Residence permit for internship for higher education 62

Summary 63

Traveling in Sweden 66
When to travel to Sweden? 66
Where to go and what to do? 67
Getting your tourist visa 68
Tourist visa for less than 90 days 70
Tourist visitor's permit for more than 90 days 71
Summary 73

Moving to a spouse or partner in Sweden 75
Getting a residence permit for a spouse or partner ... 75
Who can apply? 75
How to apply? 77
Summary 82

Where in Sweden do you want to live? 85
The capital Stockholm 85
Sweden's second-largest city Gothenburg 86
Sweden's southern city Malmö 87
The best student cities in Sweden 88
Experiencing the Swedish countryside 89
Settling down in northern Sweden 90
Summary 91

Finding the right type of accommodation 93
Renting an apartment or house 93
First-hand rentals 94
Second-hand rentals 95
Renting a place through Airbnb 95
Student accommodation 96
Buying a property 97
Summary 100

What to think about before you depart 102

- **Packing** **102**
  - What to pack? 102
  - Moving your stuff to Sweden 104
- **Health insurance** **106**
- **Bringing your pet with you** **108**
- **Utilities** **110**
- **Bank and taxes** **110**
- **Subscriptions and phone plans** **111**
- **Summary** **112**

What to think about when arriving in Sweden? **114**
- The Swedish Migration Agency **115**
- The Swedish Tax Agency **115**
- Opening a Swedish bank account **116**
- Getting a cellphone plan **119**
- Summary **121**

Acclimatizing to life in Sweden **123**
- A cash-free society **123**
  - What's Swish? 123
- Recycle and reuse **124**
- The alcohol monopoly **125**
- Drink your tap water **127**
- Cold and dark winters **127**
  - Reserved people 128
- Summary **129**

Integrating into Swedish society **131**
- Customs, culture, and characteristics **131**
  - Informality 131
  - Punctuality 132

  No shoes indoors!..132
  No bragging..132
  Taboo conversational topics 133
  Keep up to date on current affairs...133

Summary 134

Learning Swedish 135

Websites and apps 135
  SwedishPod101.com 136
  Babbel 136
  Italki 136
  Learning Swedish 137
  Duolingo 137

Swedish for immigrants 137

Summary 138

You're on your way to Sweden! 139

Useful links and resources 140

Useful numbers 140

Useful links 140
  Studying in Sweden 140
  Visa information 141
  Authorities in Sweden 141
  Learning Swedish 141
  Volunteering..142
  Job searching...142
  Websites for property listings..142
  Swedish news...143
  More information about Sweden..143

Public Holidays 144

References 145

Acknowledgements

This book is for everyone and anyone who wants to make their dream of a Swedish life come true. Because moving to a foreign country is already difficult enough, we hope that this book will help you take your first steps to a new, more exciting everyday life.

A special thank you to **Susanna Melinder**; without you, this book would have never been published. Thank you to everyone at **Taylor Literary Creations** for your support and help in everything we do, and to **Esraa Gamal** for helping this book come to life.

Foreword

So, you're moving to Sweden!

You've finally decided to move to Sweden! Yes, it is possible. In fact, people are doing it all the time. Immigration to Sweden has been increasing since 2006, and in 2016 Sweden hit its highest number of immigrants yet – 106 005 people (SCB, 2021)!

Just because you've decided to move to Sweden, it doesn't mean that you don't have any doubts or worries about this decision. Immigrating to another country is not always easy. The road to Sweden will involve bureaucratic obstacles, but that's where this book comes in! If you'd like to move to Sweden and want help understanding the process, this book is for you.

In this book, we'll go through how to get your visa. We'll go through when and where to go - and where to stay. You'll learn what to do before departing and after you've arrived. After reading this book, we hope you've found it helpful for everything you need to do and know before getting on that plane. We'll even give you some tips to help you acclimatize to life in Sweden and how to integrate into Swedish society. Don't miss our list of useful links and resources at the very back of the book.

Let's get started!

Key facts about Sweden

First of all, what do you really know about Sweden? Understanding a country is an excellent first step to take before moving anywhere. And if you want to understand Sweden, you'll need some knowledge. This book will try to guide you through the most important things you'll need to know. But first, some key facts about Sweden!

Key facts about Sweden

Population: 10,379,295
Capital: Stockholm
Main Language: Swedish
Official minority languages
- Sami
- Finnish
- Meänkieli (Tornedalen Finnish)
- Yiddish
- Romani Chib

Currency: Swedish Krona (also written kr or SEK, 1 SEK = EUR 0.098)
GDP: SEK 4,983 billion (2020)
Total area: 528,447 sq km
Time zone: GMT +1
Phone country code: +46
Internet domain: .se

(Source: Sweden.se, 2021a)

A mini dictionary for this book

Before we get started, we'd also like to introduce you to some useful Swedish words and expressions you might come across in this book or in the process of moving to Sweden. Here's a mini dictionary for you.

Allemansrätten: Literally "The Everyman's Right". It's sometimes translated into "Outdoor Access Rights" or the "Freedom to Roam". *Allemansrätten* is the right granted to everyone in Sweden to freely access nature. It includes the right to roam, ski, cycle, ride, and camp almost anywhere in Sweden. Exceptions include private gardens, the immediate vicinity of a home or land that is under cultivation.

Fika: A Swedish coffee break. *Fika* is to Swedes what afternoon tea is for Brits. It usually involves coffee, but coffee can also be replaced by other beverages. And with that, some delicious desserts or savory snacks. It's a social institution, the best way to spend time with a Swedish friend, and common practice in Swedish workplaces.

Jantelagen: The Law of Jante. This is not an actual law but a common rule in Sweden that basically stresses the idea that "You are not better than anyone else". Many Swedes that follow *Jantelagen* will avoid bragging or making themselves out to be more than they are.

Lagom: *Lagom* has been translated to "not too much, not too little, just right". *Lagom* is all about balance, and Swedes love having everything just *lagom*.

Migrationsverket: The Swedish Migration Agency. They're the ones who will grant you your visa or residence permit.

Personnummer: A personal identity number or Swedish ID number. Having a *personnummer* is the key to accessing many services in Sweden.

Sambo: Cohabiting partner. To count as *sambo*, it's not enough to simply have lived together briefly with a person during, for example, travel. Cohabiting partners are two people who live together in a type of "marriage-like" relationship.

Skatteverket: The Swedish Tax Agency. You'll come here to register when you arrive. They're the ones who will add you to the Swedish Population Register, and give you your *personummer* and Swedish ID card.

Studying in Sweden

So, you're thinking of studying in Sweden? You're not alone. Many foreign students come to Sweden for studies, and the number is increasing. In fact, there were 27 329 international student admissions to Swedish universities in 2020-21. That's 13% higher than the admissions in 2019-20 (University World News, 2020). Sweden as a country might already be more international than you think. 20% of Sweden's population is foreign-born or has a foreign-born parent (Study in Sweden, n.d.-a).

When you get to your Swedish university, you will likely find that the people around you come from different backgrounds – different countries, races, beliefs, and perspectives. And that diversity is something that Swedish society in general embraces! We welcome everyone, which leads us to our next question...

Why study in Sweden?

It's a good question! Sweden is an attractive country to study in. There are many reasons for this. There are almost 40 universities in Sweden. Out of these, many make it into top ranks globally. Some examples are Uppsala University, Lund University, and Stockholm University (Study.eu, n.d.-a).

Another reason is that there are many options for courses in English in Sweden. Sweden offers more than 1 000 English-taught programs (University World News, 2020)! Some of the more popular subjects include IT and engineering, business, and life sciences. Other areas that Swedish academia is known for include design, international relations, and human rights.

Many foreign students are also drawn to Sweden because of the country's progressive lifestyle and values. Many appreciate the focus on sustainability and equal rights, including LGBTQ rights. The fact that you can have an affordable, yet excellent education is also a plus!

Finally, did we mention the fast internet yet? No? You'll find some of the fastest internet connections in the world in Sweden. Fast internet connections are, however, the expected standard in Swedish homes. Only a few obscure places might be exceptions to this rule of thumb. Sweden currently ranks as the fifth-fastest internet service provider worldwide. Sweden also has excellent mobile data connections. All of this will come to good use when you research your thesis. Also, it will be appreciated when you're homesick and want to talk to friends and family back home.

What can I do on a student visa?

Now, you might feel clearer on whether you can study in Sweden or not. But what about what you can do while you're studying in Sweden? For example, can you work on a student visa in Sweden?

Many feel like they might need to work while studying for financial reasons. Others might want to work to get valuable experience. Many countries don't allow international students to work, but what about Sweden?

Good news! Sweden does allow you to work while studying as long as you have a residence permit, that is, your student visa (Studying in Sweden, n.d.-a). Many students find it challenging to find a part-time job in Sweden, especially if they don't speak Swedish yet. But it's definitely not impossible.

You might even be able to stay in Sweden and work after you have completed your degree. This is especially easy if you come from a country within the EU/EEA. Suppose you are from outside the EU/EEA, in that case, you can contact the Migration Agency for information on how to apply for an extension on your visa.

Who can study in Sweden?

The answer is... almost anyone! Regardless of your background or age, most people can study in Sweden. If you come from the EU/EEA, believe it or not, you don't have any visa requirements, and studying is free.

If you come from somewhere else, you'll probably need a student visa, and tuition fees may range between 80 000 and 295 000 SEK (9 326 – 34 388 USD or 7 862 – 28 990 EUR) per year (Educations.com, 2021a). Of course, you might also check if you're eligible for a scholarship so that you can study in Sweden.

The requirements for studying in Sweden are pretty basic. We'll list some general entry requirements below, depending on which level you'd like to study at. Remember that you will often have to meet degree-specific requirements. Make sure to read through the requirements for your specific program carefully.

Getting a bachelor degree

The general entry requirements for studies on a bachelor's level are (Educations.com, 2021b):

- You must have successfully completed your upper secondary education (high school education).
- You must be able to demonstrate English proficiency. The requirement for proficiency in English is the equivalent of the Swedish upper secondary course English 6.

Getting a master degree

The general entry requirements for studies on a master's level are (Educations.com, 2021b):

- You must have been awarded a bachelor's degree from an internationally recognized university.
- You must be able to demonstrate English proficiency. Each university might have different requirements of how this can be demonstrated. Some accept diplomas or proof from upper secondary studies or university studies of certain countries. Others require an internationally recognized test, for example, TOEFL or IELTS.

Getting a Ph.D.

The general entry requirements to be admitted to a Ph.D. program (Educations.com, 2021b):

- You must hold a university degree equivalent to a bachelor's degree, or at times a master's degree, focusing on the same subject as your intended field of study. You must have completed a degree thesis presenting your independent research.
- You must have a high level of English. In some cases, you might also need to know some Swedish.

Naturally, each university will also have its own program-specific entry requirements. You can usually find these on each university's website.

How to study in Sweden?

Now, let's say you are interested in moving to Sweden to study. Let's take a look at what your options are! Most students will fall into one of three categories: exchange student, studying as an adult, or language student. Let's check out each category.

Becoming an exchange student

This might be the most convenient way to study in Sweden. As an exchange student, you travel to Sweden as part of an exchange student program through your university or high school.

The benefits of being part of an exchange student program are many. First of all, it is often easier to apply and get accepted compared to applying to a program by yourself! Most arrangements are also made through your program. For example, accommodation, orientation, social activities, and more will likely already be arranged for you (Studying in Sweden, n.d.-b). Last but not least, exchange students usually don't have to pay tuition fees! This is because their studies follow an agreement between your university in your home country and the Swedish university you will be attending (Pop, 2021).

Exchange programs

One of the most extensive exchange programs that can get you to Sweden is the Erasmus Program. Who can apply to join the Erasmus program? Erasmus allows students from the European Union and Iceland, Liechtenstein, Norway, Croatia, Turkey, and Macedonia to join exchange programs. More than 20 Swedish universities are included in the Erasmus system. When you have finished your exchange program, you can transfer all your credits back to your home university. You can then complete your degree there. It is also possible to finish your degree in Sweden.

Erasmus is, however, not the only program you can choose from! Other exchange programs include the Nordplus Program and the Linnaeus-Palme program. The Nordplus program allows most students in the Nordic and Baltic countries to study at universities in this region. The Linnaeus-Palme program helps students in developing countries to get an education. Programs such as these are one of the reasons why you can find such great diversity at Swedish universities!

How to apply for an exchange program?

So, how do you apply for an exchange program? And what if you don't live in any of the countries included in these three programs? First of all, don't worry, these are only three examples.

If you are interested in studying in Sweden as an exchange student, what is the first step? The easiest first step would be to contact the international studies office or exchange student office at your university. They'll know best whether your country is included in an exchange program that can send you to Sweden.

Studying as an adult

But maybe becoming an exchange student isn't for you? Perhaps you'd like more freedom and independence? Then this section is for you. If you want to study independently as an adult, you can apply for a university program or course yourself. People who apply for a higher education program on their own are often called Free Movers.

Independence = Responsibility

Applying on your own requires more work! If you are a Free Mover, you will have to do a lot of research. If you need funding, you will also have to secure it yourself. You will also have to make a lot of arrangements yourself, for example for your visa. There will be more information on how to get your student visa below!

It is also essential to know that it is much harder to be admitted when you apply independently. Many international students apply for Swedish programs each year. You have to work hard, do well in your studies and show potential. And your application will have to reflect that. It is hard work, but it is far from impossible!

How to apply as a Free Mover?

So, where do you get started? First of all, you'll have to decide which universities and programs you're interested in. This involves researching which universities provide the program you are interested in and weighing their pros and cons. You can search for programs you are interested in through Universityadmissions.se. Many universities also have strong social media presences, which can be a fantastic way to learn about the university. Some might have online platforms or online Q&A sessions where you can ask questions about student life, admissions, and more.

When you have decided where you want to apply, you can proceed with your application on Universityadmissions.com. In many countries, you apply directly to the university or college. In Sweden, however, you make your general application for all the schools you are interested in through this website. Apart from your general application, some universities also require that you send a separate application for the program you are applying to. On Universityadmissions.com, your first step is to create an account. The site will then take you through the entire admission process.

Don't forget to apply in time! Suppose you are applying for the fall semester; in that case, your application usually has to be completed by mid-January (Studying in Sweden, n.d.-b). However, this can vary from university to university. Therefore, it's always important to double-check the deadline and make sure you hand in your application on time.

If you apply for the fall semester, you will get your admission notices in March. If you apply for the spring semester, your admission notices should arrive in November. This gives you time to make the necessary plans! There is only a limited number of programs that start in the spring semester. If you're planning on applying for a one-year program that is available to start in spring, you might want to consider starting at this time. Why? Beginning in the spring will allow you to spend all summer in Sweden – which many consider the country's best season.

Becoming a language student

Many who move to Sweden to study will try to learn a bit of the language. But you might not be one of them. This section is for those of you who want to go to Sweden specifically to learn Swedish.

Perhaps you are passionate about linguistics and want to know more about the exciting Scandinavian languages. Maybe you have a Swedish family connection and want to be able to communicate with relatives or connect with your roots. Or, perhaps you're planning to move to and settle down in Sweden and want to get a head start by mastering the language first. Learning Swedish is an instrumental first step if you wish to find a job in Sweden or integrate into Swedish society.

Many find Swedish to be a language that sounds beautifully melodic. This is because it has an interesting inflection and intonation. Just like English, Swedish is a Germanic language. Therefore, English speakers will likely find some similarities with English when it comes to vocabulary and grammar structure.

Many do, however, find Swedish a relatively complex language to learn and pronounce. But with the right course, you'll find the way of learning Swedish that fits you the best. Let's go through some methods of studying Swedish in Sweden!

Swedish language studies at university

First of all, let's talk about university. This suits you if you're interested in really going deep and getting a profound understanding of the Swedish language. Some universities provide study abroad Swedish language programs.

Just one example is Lund University, one of the high-ranking Swedish universities we mentioned earlier. They have two Swedish as a foreign language programs: a one-semester program and a two-semester program (Lund University, 2021). The one-semester program covers Swedish as a foreign language, levels 1-4, while the two-semester program covers levels 1-8.

If you complete level 8, you meet the language proficiency requirement to apply for Swedish-taught studies at Swedish universities. So, if you are interested in Swedish-taught studies, this is an excellent way to get your Swedish up to that level!

Basic requirements for this sort of program are basic eligibility for university studies and proficiency in English (Lund University, n.d.). You will likely need to send in a higher secondary school diploma and transcript and proof of English proficiency, such as a TOEFL or IELTS certificate.

Cultural immersion programs

Another way to study is through language immersion programs. These are most often tied to American-based universities (Go Overseas, n.d.-a). This sort of program will usually cover speaking, listening, writing, and reading. They can also cover activities that are culturally and historically significant.

The programs are often quite intense, covering 15-20 hours of language studies per week. This type of studying can be a good fit for you if you want to really plunge in and learn about the Swedish language and culture for a short period of time. If the program is tied to a university, earning and transferring university credits is generally straightforward.

Homestays in Sweden

A homestay is similar to a cultural immersion program. It's also an intense program with 15 to 30 lessons per week (Go Overseas, n.d.-a). With a homestay, you also have a very immersive experience, or maybe even more so!

When you participate in a homestay program, you learn Swedish while living with a Swedish host family. This allows you to truly experience the language and culture firsthand. It will give you a more intimate insight into Swedish everyday life.

The program duration can be anything from one week up to two months. However, these programs do not necessarily allow you to obtain university credits. If credits are important to you, make sure that you double-check this in advance.

With this type of program, you will also likely need to make your own arrangements for travel and visa. So, if you are simply looking for a quick trip to Sweden with a short and intense program to learn Swedish, this could be the perfect experience for you!

Getting your student visa

Have you finally gotten your acceptance letter? How exciting! You can finally start planning your trip to Sweden. One of the first things you'll probably think about is how to get a visa.

Kind in mind, this is the order you should be doing things in. First, you apply to the program or course. Only *after* you've received your acceptance letter should you start putting specific plans into action, like applying for your visa. Naturally, you can do as much research as you wish in advance. Still, you will need your acceptance letter for actual arrangements, such as applying for a visa.

When you're studying abroad, one crucial step is always to look up the visa situation. So, do you need a student visa to study in Sweden? The answer is that it depends! In general, it depends on two factors: 1) where you are from, and 2) how long you are staying.

EU/EEA countries and Nordic countries

If you are legally living in an EU/EEA country, then congratulations! You can reside in Sweden for work or studies without applying for a student visa or a residence permit (Studying in Sweden, n.d.-c)! You do, however, need to register your presence in the country with the Migration Agency within the first 90 days. We'd recommend that you make an appointment as soon as possible, as wait times can be long.

If you stay in Sweden for over a year, you also need to register with the Swedish Population Register. You can do so at *Skatteverket*, the Swedish Tax Agency. When you do this, you will receive a *personnummer*, a personal identity number. So, if you are going to Sweden to study a lengthier program of over a year, you will require this. As we will get into in our "Arriving in Sweden" section, having a *personnummer* is the key to accessing many services in Sweden. It's therefore wise to register with *Skatteverket* as soon as possible.

Are you a legal resident and/or citizen of a Nordic country? All you need do is let the Swedish Migration Agency know that you are in the country for studies (Studying in Sweden, n.d.-c). This is relatively easy. You only need to send them your acceptance letter and proof that you live in a Nordic country.

Non-EU/EEA countries

What if you're not from an EU/EEA or a Nordic country? Not to fret. This is where student visas and residence permits come into the picture! What is the difference between a student visa and a residence permit?

You get **a student visa** when you are a non-EU/EEA citizen who plans to study and stay in Sweden for less than 90 days. You get a **residence permit** when you are a non-EU/EEA citizen who plans to study and stay in Sweden for more than 90 days.

Requirements

Let's get right into it! What requirements do you need to fulfill when applying for a student visa or residence permit (Lungu, 2021)? These are some of the requirements:

- You have to have received your acceptance letter or proof that you have been admitted.
- Your university study program has to be full-time.
- You have to have comprehensive health insurance if you stay less than one year.
- Your passport has to be valid for a minimum of six months past the date of your arrival to Sweden.
- If there is tuition to be paid, it is recommended for you to have paid the first tuition fee.

Another essential requirement is regarding your finances. You will also be required to show that you can support yourself financially during your studies. You can either show that you already have enough money to last you through your study period or that you're able to earn money during that time. One way to show this is through a bank statement.

How much money you are required to show proof of can depend on many factors. For example, whether you are bringing a spouse or children, have free housing in Sweden, have a scholarship or other financial aid, and so on. The living expense requirement can also change with time, so make sure to look up the current requirements. In 2021, the requirement was to have at least 8 568 SEK (999 USD or 842 EUR) per month (Migrationsverket, 2021a).

What will be included in your application? Here is a list of some of the documents that are often required:

- 2 copies of your passport.
- Minimum 2 photos for your passport.
- Acceptance letter to the school you have been accepted to, plus a copy.
- 2 copies of your current degrees and diplomas
- Various proof of financial means. This can include financial aid, loans, grants, scholarships, free housing arrangements, bank statements, credit statements, etc. Don't worry about converting bank statements and credit statements to SEK, as this is not required.

Finally, don't forget to look up the exact visa requirements for the country you live in! The easiest way to do this is often to get in contact with the embassy in your country. You can find the embassy of your country on SwedenAbroad.com. You can also contact Migrationsverket, the Swedish

Migration Agency, through their website Migrationsverket.se. Their website is also where you will be able to find applications and other information you might need.

A permit will often be valid for 365 days or less (Studying in Sweden, n.d.-c). That is, the permit will expire within 365 days. This means that you will have to renew your permit every year! Your local Swedish Migration Agency office will help you with renewal information so you can reapply for your visa.

If you receive a residence permit, you might still have to consider a visa. If you come from a country that needs an entry visa to travel into Sweden, then you will have to be photographed and fingerprinted at your embassy or general consulate (Migrationsverket, 2021a). After this, a permit card will be made, which you might have to present when you enter Sweden.

If your country does not require an entry visa for Sweden, you can be photographed and fingerprinted after your arrival in Sweden (Migrationsverket, 2021a). You can do so by making an appointment at *Migrationsverket*, the Swedish Migration Agency. Make sure to have an actual address in Sweden before doing this. This is because you can't change the address your card will be sent to after the order has been made. So, if you're couch-hopping for a while, make sure you write an address where you will definitely be able to receive the documents.

Now you have the basic information necessary to get to Sweden and stay there as a student! We hope you enjoy your studies and learn a lot – both inside and outside of the classroom.

Summary

Basically, anyone can study in Sweden! One of the beautiful things about studying in Sweden is the diversity of people living and studying there. People of all ages, backgrounds, races, beliefs, and perspectives are welcome. Requirements and costs may vary depending on where you come from, but generally, the requirements are pretty basic. Do you need or want to work while studying? The possibility to work on a student visa is another benefit of being a student in Sweden.

Many of Sweden's universities make it into top ranks globally, and there are many options for English-language tuition! As an English speaker with no Swedish skills, you'll still be able to choose from more than 1000 English-taught programs. Whether you are interested in IT, business, or human rights, Sweden will have a program for you.

If you go to Sweden to study, you will likely fall into one of three categories: Exchange student, studying as an adult, or language student!

Being an exchange student is likely the most convenient way of studying in Sweden. An exchange program will help you with most of the arrangements. Also, it is easier to apply and get accepted to a program when you are an exchange student. What can you do if you want to find out which exchange programs are available for you? The best way is to contact the exchange student office at your university.

If you choose to be a Free Mover, that is, to study as an adult, you will be more independent. You will also have more responsibilities, like doing research, applying on your own, and making the necessary arrangements.

We'll be honest; compared to exchange students, it will be harder for you to get admitted. But it is not impossible! When you have decided on a university, you can apply through Universityadmissions.se.

As a language student, you want to go to Sweden specifically to learn Swedish! One way of doing so is by applying for Swedish language studies at a university in Sweden. In the Swedish language program of one university, you can choose between learning Swedish levels 1-4 during one semester or levels 1-4 during two semesters. You can also learn Swedish through a cultural immersion program or a homestay. These kinds of programs allow you to learn Swedish during a shorter and more intense period of time.

After you've gotten your acceptance letter, you can start applying for a visa. But wait, if you are a resident in an EU/EEA country, you don't need a student visa or residence permit! There might still be some paperwork, so make sure you still have everything that is required.

If you are from a non-EU/EEA country, you will likely have to apply for a student visa or a residence permit. If you're going to study and stay in Sweden for less than 90 days and need a visa to enter Sweden, you will need to apply for a student visa. If you wish to study and stay in Sweden for longer than 90 days, you have to apply for a residence permit.

Make sure you fulfill the requirements before you apply. For example, make sure that your passport is valid for a minimum of 6 months. Also make sure you have all the required documents and copies for the application. This includes copies of your passport, passport photos, acceptance letter, diplomas, and proof of financial means.

Working in Sweden

Has working in Sweden been on your mind for a while? Well, it's time to do something about it! Going to Sweden for work is a popular option and very doable.

Perhaps you've heard that Sweden has an outstanding balance between work and personal life. Many Swedes would confirm that there is some truth to that. So, let's get into it. Why do so many people want to move to Sweden for work?

Why work in Sweden?

1. Globalization

One reason is how globalization drives Sweden forward. Sweden ambitiously tries to stay ahead of global competition. The result of this is that Sweden's business environment is very dynamic, with exciting new startups successfully opening up new roads. Talent, including international talent, is in high demand, and you can be among that talent!

Because of Sweden's global perspective, working in Sweden is possible even if you only speak English. This is good news for you if you find the thought of learning Swedish scary. For example, tech companies have a high demand for new talent (Sweden.se, 2021b). They often look abroad for new hires. The tech industry is growing rapidly, and the Swedish workforce alone can't fill this demand. More prominent international companies are also more likely to sponsor work permits for people with the right skills. In general, however, it can be tough to find a job in Sweden without knowing the language.

Even if you don't speak Swedish, most people you meet on the street will be able to communicate with you in English. And people in a workplace with a more global outlook will likely have a higher English proficiency. That said, if you do decide to learn Swedish, we doubt that you'll regret it! It'll vastly improve your chances of finding work. It'll be helpful in your daily life in Sweden and will be an essential step towards integrating into Swedish society.

2. Innovation

We already mentioned that Sweden has many successful and exciting new startups. This is not surprising, as Sweden is known for valuing innovation! Children are encouraged to think outside the box and create new solutions for old problems early in school. Sweden has been placed as one of the world's most innovative nations by the European Commission's European Innovation Scoreboard (MediCarrera, n.d.).

Many Swedish companies have taken their fields to the next level. Some examples are Ericsson, IKEA, Mojang, and Spotify. And if you work within areas related to energy and ICT, you're in luck. Companies within such fields are at the cutting edge of technological advancement and sustainable development in Sweden. If you want to unleash your out-of-the-box thinking, no matter which industry you're in, Sweden is an excellent place to do it.

3. Sustainability

Speaking of sustainable development, Sweden is all about it. Swedish companies often promote sustainability. Sweden is a country with beautiful nature in abundance, so it's no surprise that its residents are often passionate about protecting it.

However, when we say sustainability, we're not just talking about the environment. Sustainability also involves working against corruption and safeguarding what is most precious to humanity, like human rights and equality.

4. Equality

There is no place on Earth with a perfect system for equality. That said, Sweden really tries to be a country where people have as high a chance as possible to be treated equally.

No matter which country you're from, your gender, religion, or the sexual orientation you identify with – Sweden's goal is that you will be treated fairly. The country's anti-discrimination legislation tries to ensure this (Sweden.se, 2021b).

Sweden's low gender gap is just one example of this. Having closed more than 81% of its overall gender gap, Sweden is placed 4th on the World Economic Forum's Gender Gap Index 2016 (MediCarrera, n.d.). And who doesn't want to be treated fairly and equally in the workplace?

5. Balanced life

Last but not least, there's that balance we mentioned in the introduction. One of the most famous Swedish words is "*lagom*", and it's a word that genuinely reflects Swedish values. *Lagom* has been translated as meaning "not too much, not too little, just right". *Lagom* is all about balance, and Swedes love having everything just *lagom*. This is also true about their workplace.

So, it's no surprise that Sweden has a good balance between work and personal life. There's also a good balance between professionalism and a friendly, casual environment in the workplace in Sweden. And no matter how busy you are, there is always time for a "*fika*" break. *Fika* is another popular and well-known Swedish word. It's basically a coffee break, often with something sweet on the side. We can't stress enough how much Swedes love their coffee - and their *fika*. A *fika* break is generally included in the work time of employees. But it's more than just a coffee break; it gives you time to refocus, to take a break from work, stretch your legs and chat with your coworkers.

So, people expect you to do your job, but they also expect you to have a life outside of it. That means you'll have time to enjoy the beautiful nature and other pleasant aspects of living in Sweden – which is another benefit in itself.

And you can really enjoy Swedish nature. Why? Because of *Allemansrätten* (Visit Sweden, 2021). *Allemansrätten* (Outdoor Access Rights) is a special right that everyone in Sweden has. It's the freedom to roam. You have the right to roam, ski, cycle, ride, and camp almost anywhere in Sweden. The only exceptions are private gardens, places near a home or land that is under cultivation. So, the Swedish countryside is your oyster. You're free to go and explore the Swedish Lapland, the archipelago, or the beautiful forests. In our section "Useful links and resources", you can find a link to more information about the exact rules that apply!

Finally, just a note on paydays, vacation days, and parental leave in Sweden. Salaries are generally paid monthly, the most common payday being the 25th of each month. Not necessarily a pro or a con of working in Sweden, but we figured you might want to know. When it comes to vacation, Swedes are entitled to at least 25 full days of paid leave every year. If you are working part-time, your yearly vacation is recalculated to the equivalent of 25 days. Swedes are also entitled to 480 days of paid parental leave when they have a child. Each parent is entitled to 240 of those days. You'll find a list of Swedish public holidays under the "Useful links and resources" section at the very back of the book. These public holidays are often called *röda dagar* in Swedish, which means "red days".

Are you convinced? If you've decided that Sweden might just be the place for you, what's the next step? Well, it depends on how you're planning to find a job in Sweden. In the following section, we'll look at four ways many people find work in Sweden. We'll look at the possibilities of a working holiday, a company transfer, and independently looking for a job.

A one-year working holiday

What is a working holiday? Isn't a "holiday" the opposite of "working"? Well, not in this case. A working holiday is a program that allows young people from certain countries to stay and work in Sweden for up to one year (Migrationsverket, 2021b).

The working holiday program aims to give young people the opportunity to work in Sweden while experiencing the Swedish lifestyle and culture. You do not have to have an employment offer when you apply for this type of residence permit. You can start your job hunt once you've arrived in Sweden.

If you are going to Sweden on a working holiday, you'll have to apply for a permit to stay in Sweden. It's essential to be aware that a working holiday permit can't be extended past the one year it is valid. So, if you already know that you are interested in going to Sweden more long-term, this might not be the option for you. It's usually not possible to apply for a different visa or permit from Sweden when your working holiday permit is about to expire. Likely, you will have to apply for another permit after you've left Sweden. It's also a requirement that you're not physically in Sweden when you receive a new residence permit.

Who can apply for the working holiday program?

Who are these "young people" we are referring to? 18 to 30 years old is the age limit for obtaining a work holiday permit. Does that mean that as long as you are between 18 and 30, you can apply? Not necessarily.

These working holidays are only possible because Sweden has entered into agreements with certain countries (Migrationsverket, 2021b). Therefore, it's only an option for you if you come from one of those countries. So, which countries are included in these agreements?

Below, we will include a list of countries that have an agreement with Sweden for working holiday programs. However, this list is not necessarily set in stone. So, before making plans, you must make sure that the country you live in still has an agreement with Sweden!

You may be able to apply for a working holiday if you are a citizen of:

- Argentina
- Australia
- Canada
- Chile
- Hong Kong
- Japan
- New Zealand
- South Korea
- Uruguay

Requirements for a working holiday residence permit

What are the requirements to obtain a residence permit for a working holiday?

According to Migrationsverket (2021b), you have to:

- Be a resident of Argentina, Australia, Canada, Hong Kong, Japan, New Zealand, South Korea, or Uruguay
- Be between 18 and 30 years of age
- Have enough money to provide for yourself initially in Sweden (minimum 15 000 SEK, which at the time of writing corresponds to approximately 1 749 USD and 1 474 EURO)
- Have a return ticket or sufficient money to buy one
- Have a valid passport that will not expire during your stay in Sweden
- Have comprehensive health insurance that will cover healthcare when you're in Sweden (this requirement does not apply to Australian citizens)
- Not have accompanying children
- In most cases, pay a fee (at the time of writing, the cost to apply for the residence permit is 1 500 SEK, approximately 175 USD or 147 EURO)

We'll cover how you can apply for a residence permit for a working holiday under the "Getting your work visa" section, so stay tuned.

Company transfers

What about if you're coming to Sweden as part of a company transfer? If you are an EU citizen, things will go smoothly! As an EU citizen, you have the right to work in Sweden without a residence permit (InterNations GO!, 2019).

But what if you're a citizen of a country outside the EU/EEA and Switzerland? And you're employed by a company outside of EU/EEA? Then Sweden's ICT permit is for you.

What is an ICT permit? An ICT permit allows you the right to travel to and stay in Sweden, as you work at a company in Sweden within the same corporate group as the host company.

Who can apply for an ICT permit?

ICT stands for "Intra-Corporate Transfer" and is applicable to you if you're employed at a company outside the EU/EEA and are going to get transferred to the company's branch in Sweden (Migrationsverket, 2021c).

There are three main categories for who can receive an ICT permit. You have to be a manager, a specialist, or a trainee. A manager has a leadership position and can, for example, be the head of a department within the company. A specialist has valuable knowledge and a high level of qualification and experience. A trainee is internally relocated for career development or to obtain training.

Requirements for an ICT permit

What are the requirements to be eligible for an intra-corporate transfer permit?

According to Migrationsverket (2021c), you have to:

- Serve in the position of manager, specialist, or trainee at the company in Sweden for over 90 days
- Have a passport that is valid and will not expire during the time of your permit

- Have the professional qualifications, experience, or training required for your position as manager, specialist, or trainee
- Have an employment contract with your employer outside the EU/EEA and a trainee agreement if your position is as a trainee
- Have been employed for a minimum of three months without interruption at the time of relocation
- Be able to verify qualifications needed to practice the profession in Sweden if it concerns a regulated profession
- Be able to move to a company in a country outside the EU after the period of relocation

One of the points mentions an employment contract and a trainee agreement. These have to be translated into Swedish or English and include the following information:

- Your employer's name and address (outside the EEA)
- Your (the employee's) name and address
- When your employment began
- The city where your training or work will take place
- A brief description of your duties
- Your salary and payroll benefits
- Your job title or professional designation, or whether you are a trainee

These are the requirements for you. But wait, there's more! There are also things that your employer will need to do.

Your employer has to:

- Create an employment offer for you
- Offer you compensation according to what is customary in the industry or on the level of the Swedish collective agreements or higher
- Offer you terms of employment on the same level as employees posted in Sweden or higher
- Offer employment that enables you to support yourself

Independently looking for work

What if you're not moving to Sweden through a company transfer? Maybe you just want to move to and work in Sweden but don't have a specific way of doing this yet? Can you move to Sweden to independently look for work?

The answer is, again, that it depends on where you come from. Are you from an EU/EEA country? Let's start there!

Residents of EU/EEA countries

As mentioned, EU/EEA residents have a right to residence in Sweden and do not need permission to live and work here. This means that you can move to Sweden even if you don't have a job and spend some time looking for one. You can also choose to start and operate a private business in Sweden. All you will need is a valid passport or ID card that shows your citizenship (Migrationsverket, 2021d).

When you arrive, you might visit Arbetsförmedlingen, the Swedish Public Employment Service. They can help you if you need assistance with your job hunting. Some have found it a bit of a challenge to get help without a Swedish ID card, but it is supposedly possible! You can also look for work in their job portal Platsbanken. Other job portals you can use are The Local, Swedish Jobs, and Neuvoo.

Residents of non-EU/EEA countries

What about if you're from outside the EU/EEA? If you want to come to Sweden for work, you have to have a work and residence permit before entering Sweden (Arbetsförmedlingen, n.d.). To get a permit, you need an offer of employment in Sweden. Unfortunately, this means that you can't come to Sweden to *look for* a job. You have to have secured your job *before* applying for your work permit (Migrationsverket, 2021e).

This doesn't mean that you can't move to Sweden for work. It simply means that you will have to find a job before moving there! You might do this by searching online job portals or by contacting a recruitment agency. A few useful websites for your job search are The Local, Swedish Jobs, and Neuvoo. Naturally, if you already have your eye on a position in a Swedish company, you might apply directly. If you have your aim set on one of Sweden's multinational companies, you might want to look up their contact details on Business Sweden's website.

According to Migrationsverket (2021f), there are certain occupations where special rules apply. So, if your work in Sweden falls under one of the following categories, it might be worth checking out any special rules that might apply to you. One of these occupations is being an au pair. If you are interested in moving to Sweden as an au pair, we will go through the work permit requirements for au pairs in the section "Getting your work visa".

Occupations to which special rules apply:

- Performer
- Au pair
- Berry picker
- Seasonal work
- Researcher
- Athlete/coach
- Trainee
- Volunteer

Digital nomad/remote work

A new type of visa that is starting to show up in more and more countries worldwide is a digital nomad visa. This type of visa is sometimes called a "remote work visa" or "freelancer visa". This type of visa is for remote workers who travel regularly and keep working online using modern technology.

Unfortunately, Sweden does not at this time have a digital nomad visa in place. If you are a digital nomad, it won't be as convenient to move to Sweden as countries with digital nomad visas.

Applying for a job

We'd also want to say a quick word or two on resumés and personal letters. A resumé is called a CV in Swedish. You probably know how to write a resumé; list your education, experience, and add your contact information and maybe a summary. Try to highlight the more important information rather than including absolutely everything. A tip for applying for a job in Sweden is to really try to make your resumé stand out. Swedish resumés will also often include a picture of the applicant. You can find some helpful Swedish resumé and personal letter templates online.

What if you've found a job and have gotten an employment offer? Well, then it's time to obtain a work permit and residence permit. More on that below, in the section "Getting your work visa".

Getting your work visa

Now it's time to figure out your visa situation! What kind of visa do you need, and how do you apply? This all depends on the way you're moving to Sweden for work. We've mentioned a few different categories and ways of working in Sweden. Let's look through some of those categories and get into how you can apply for your work permit.

Getting your working holiday residence permit

You will need to apply for a residence permit if you are interested in going to Sweden on a working holiday. The requirements have already been mentioned, but how do you apply?

The easiest way to obtain a residence permit for a working holiday is to apply through the Migration Agency's e-service (Migrationsverket, 2021b). What are the requirements to use the e-service? You need to have:

- Copies of your passport and the pages that show personal data, photo, signature, passport number, the issuing country, the passport's validity period, and whether you have permission to live in another country than your home country
- A copy of a return ticket or a statement showing you have the funds to buy one
- A bank statement showing that you can support yourself when you arrive in Sweden
- Documents that show you have necessary health insurance (not applicable to Australian citizens)

If you can't apply online, you will have to fill in a form and submit it to a Swedish embassy or consulate general. The form has the number 155011 on it, and is called "Application for working holiday visa for young people". It can be downloaded from the Migration Agency's website.

Remember that you cannot enter Sweden until you have your permit. After submitting your application, you can check your application on the Migration Agency's website.

Getting your ICT permit

When you are moving to Sweden through a company transfer, you have to obtain an ICT permit. The easiest way to apply is through the e-service on the Migration Agency's website (Migrationsverket, 2021c).

However, the person to start the e-service is not you, the employee. The person who starts the e-service is your employer, who will email you a link leading you to the e-service. The application fee for the permit is SEK 2 000 (233 USD or 197 EUR).

Here are other requirements for using the e-service:

- You need to be able to pay the application fee by card
- You need copies of specific pages of your passport
- You need a union declaration
- You need an employment contract from your employer
- If you are a trainee, you need a degree certificate and a trainee agreement

You must receive a decision before you travel to Sweden. A decision on an ICT permit is made within 90 days.

You generally collect the decision at the embassy or consulate-general you stated in the application. The decision can, in some cases, also be sent out by email. If your application is approved, you will receive a residence permit card!

You might need an entry visa to travel to Sweden. If you do, you will have to visit a Swedish embassy or consulate-general to be photographed and fingerprinted as soon as possible. If you don't need a visa to travel to Sweden, you will still need to be photographed and fingerprinted, but you can do so at the Migration Agency after you arrive in Sweden.

Getting your "independent" work and resident permit

Are you from outside the EU/EEA but managed to find work in Sweden? First of all, congratulations! As we have mentioned, people from outside the EU/EEA need an offer of employment before applying for a work permit (Migrationsverket, 2021e).

There is another requirement for you and your employer to be aware of. Your employer has to have advertised the job position in Sweden, the EU/EEA, and Switzerland for at least ten days before your offer of employment was made. Your employer can do this in the Swedish Public Employment Service (Arbetsförmedlingen) job bank. The advertisements in the job bank of *Arbetsförmedlingen* will also be visible in the European job bank EURES (Migrationsverket, 2021g).

This is the application process for a work permit:

1. Your employer initiates the work permit application by creating and completing an employment offer on the Migration Agency's website. The offer has to include your name, birth date, education, citizenship, and email address.
2. When the offer of employment is completed, you will receive an email with instructions on how to apply for

the work permit. Don't forget to double-check that the employment terms mentioned in the offer are correct. If your family is moving with you, you apply for their permits at the same time too.

3. You will need to enclose documents with the application. For example, you will need scanned or photographed copies of specific pages of your passport. If you have a representative, you will also need a power of attorney. If your family is moving with you, you will need documents related to them as well.
4. You pay a fee using Visa or Mastercard, and then you can submit the application.
5. The Migration Agency will process your application, and they will contact you if any further information is needed.

If your permit is granted, and it's for more than three months, you will receive a residence permit card. If you don't need an entry visa to travel to Sweden, you can submit the necessary information to get a residence permit card once you've arrived in Sweden. You can do that at the Migration Agency.

If you do need an entry visa to travel to Sweden, you will have to contact a Swedish Embassy or consulate-general. You and any family accompanying you to Sweden will have to go there to be photographed and fingerprinted as soon as possible.

Getting your au pair work permit

Finally, there are some occupations where there are special rules for the work permits. One of those occupations is as an au pair in Sweden. Let us go through the requirements and steps!

If you are a non-EU citizen, you will need a residence permit. Citizens of certain countries may also need a visa if the work lasts for less than three months. The motive of going to Sweden as an au pair should be to increase your knowledge of Sweden and your language skills.

According to Migrationsverket (2021h), to fulfill the requirements for getting a residence permit as an au pair, you have to:

- Have a work agreement with a family in Sweden, stating that you will do light household work for no more than 25 hours per week (household work time and study time may not exceed a total of 40 hours per week)
- Be at least 18 years old and under the age of 30 when the decision is made
- have a passport that will not expire during the time of the permit
- Have applied for comprehensive health insurance, which is valid in Sweden
- Have enough money to stay in Sweden and pay for your ticket home
- In most cases, pay a fee of 1 500 SEK (175 USD or 147 EUR)
- Not have family members that accompany you

The application is made online through an e-service on the Migration Agency's website. The e-service is started by the employer, in this case, the host family you will be staying with. They will get the e-service started and then email you a link where you can access it.

The requirements for you to use the e-service are that you have to:

- Have received the email from your host family that leads you to the service
- Have copies of the relevant pages of your passport
- Have a written agreement from your host family with the terms of your employment
- Have a certificate that you have applied for, or already have comprehensive health insurance which is valid in Sweden

If your permit is for more than three months, you will receive a residence permit card after your permit is granted. If you don't need an entry visa to travel to Sweden, you can book an appointment to go the Migration Agency once you've arrived in Sweden. You can submit the necessary information to get a residence permit card at this time.

If you need an entry visa to travel to Sweden, you will have to contact a Swedish Embassy or consulate-general as soon as possible. You will have to go there to be photographed and fingerprinted.

What about if you want to switch host families while in Sweden? Do you have to submit a new application? No, as long as your permit is valid and the requirements for a residence permit are still met, you won't have to submit a new application.

Summary

There are many benefits to working in Sweden. Some of the reasons why people choose to move to Sweden for work are the level of globalization and innovation in the country and the high focus on sustainability. Many people are also attracted to how highly equality is valued in Sweden or the work-life balance Swedes enjoy.

In this section, we've looked at three main ways of working in Sweden: A working holiday program, a company transfer, and independently looking for work.

First of all, if you are an EU/EEA citizen, you have the right to work in Sweden without a residence permit. Things will go smoothly for you! But let's dive into it a bit deeper for our friends outside the EU/EEA.

The working holiday program is a program that allows young people between the age of 18 and 30 to move to Sweden (and other countries) and search for a job there. You can look for a job in Sweden while simultaneously getting the chance to experience the Swedish lifestyle for up to one year. To qualify for the working holiday visa, your country has to be one of the countries that have an agreement with Sweden for working holiday programs. If you fulfill the requirements and plan to go to Sweden on a working holiday, you'll need a residence permit. The easiest way to apply is through the Migration Agency's e-service.

If you wish to come to Sweden as part of a company transfer, you'll need an ICT permit. ICT stands for "Intra/Corporate transfer". This permit applies to you if you're employed at a company outside the EU/EEA and will be transferred to the company's branch in Sweden. You have to be a manager, a specialist, or a trainee to qualify. To obtain your ICT permit, your employer will have to start your application using the e-service on the Migration Agency's website. Your employer will then send you a link to continue the application through the e-service.

Now, let's talk about looking for work in Sweden independently. If you're an EU/EEA resident, you are free to move to Sweden and look for a job. However, if you're not from an EU/EEA country, you need a work permit before entering Sweden. You will have to look for a job, find a job, and secure it before applying to move to Sweden! A few helpful job portals are The Local, Swedish Jobs, and Neuvoo. An essential requirement is that your employer must have advertised the job position in Sweden, the EU/EEA, and Switzerland for a minimum of ten days before you're offered the job. After that, your employer can start your work permit application by completing an employment offer on the Migration Agency's website. Be aware that special work permit rules apply for certain occupations, such as working as an au pair. Make sure to check if your occupation is one of them.

Religious activities in Sweden

Perhaps you are thinking of going to Sweden for religious purposes? You will be happy to know that there are visa options for visitors who wish to do so. The two options depend on how long you want to stay in Sweden.

If you'd like to visit for less than 90 days, you can apply for a visa to visit Sweden for religious purposes. If you want to visit Sweden for more than 90 days, you can apply for a visitor's permit for religious purposes. These two types of visas might be used by, for example, monks, nuns, or missionaries. We'll get into the requirements for these two options below, in the section "Getting your religious activities visa".

Religion in Sweden

If you are visiting Sweden for religious purposes, you're probably curious about religion in Sweden. Truth be told, Sweden is a very secular nation, being numbered among the least religious countries in the world. This might make Sweden an intimidating, but also a perfect place for say, a missionary to travel to.

According to a survey, almost half of Swedes said religion is "not important". Only about 20% of Swedes said that religion was "very important" or "somewhat important" (Sweden.se, 2021c).

Svenska kyrkan (The Church of Sweden) is Evangelical Lutheran. The church has been separated from the state since the year 2000. This means that Sweden doesn't have an official state church.

The most visible way religion exists in Swedes' lives is during holidays, cultural traditions, and traditional rituals. This includes, for example, christenings, funerals, and marriages. However, more and more people are pursuing non-religious forms of rituals. As an example, only 24% of weddings in Sweden are officiated by Svenska kyrkan.

After Svenska kyrkan, other prominent Christian churches are "*frikyrkor*" (Free Churches). These churches are also protestant but independent of Svenska kyrkan.

Sweden also has a Jewish community. Religious diversity is increasing with increased immigration. Because of this, there are also many country-specific Eastern Orthodox churches, such as the Syrian Orthodox Church. Islam is another growing religion in Sweden.

Sweden has become highly secular, but is also very tolerant. Freedom of religion has been part of Swedish law since 1951. According to studies, a vast majority of Swedes also believe that everyone should have the right to freely practice their religion.

Getting your religious activities visa

Now let's get into *how* to visit Sweden for religious purposes. As mentioned, the requirements differ depending on if you're staying for less than 90 days or more than 90 days. Let's look through the options one at a time.

Getting your visa to visit Sweden for religious purposes

This is the best option if you want to visit Sweden for less than 90 days (Migrationsverket, 2021i). What are the basic requirements for receiving a visa for visiting Sweden for religious purposes?

To receive this type of visa, you have to:

- Have an invitation from a religious assembly or organization
- Describe the purpose of your visit to Sweden
- Have a passport that has at least two empty pages, was issued within the last ten years, and is valid for at least three months after the visa has expired
- Have enough money to support yourself and pay for your return trip home (You are required to have 450 SEK per day of stay in Sweden, which is around 52 USD or 44 EUR)
- Have individual medical travel insurance which covers all costs that might arise (it must be valid for all Schengen countries and cover costs of a minimum of 30 000 EUR, which is around 35 600 USD)
- Show that you intend to leave the Schengen area on the last day before your visa expires
- A photograph in passport format which is not older than six months

Is that all? Not necessarily. The embassy might require other documents as well. It is, therefore, important that you contact your embassy to verify what applies to you specifically.

How to apply?

So, let's say you fulfill all the requirements. How do you apply? Most people apply for this type of visa through an external service provider. The external service provider can be a company that provides support services to people applying for a visa, for example, a visa agency. You can find out about potential agreements with external service providers by visiting your embassy's website.

If there isn't an agreement between your embassy and an external service provider, you can apply directly at the embassy. If you do, you will have to hand in form number 119031 (Application for Schengen Visa). You can download this form from the Migration Agency's website (Migrationsverket, 2021i).

You can also apply through an e-service if you are applying from one of the following three embassies:

- Sweden's embassy in Seoul, South Korea
- Sweden's embassy in Teheran, Iran
- Sweden's embassy in Tokyo, Japan

After you have submitted your application, you will usually receive an answer within the next two weeks. However, if you haven't received a response after two weeks, don't panic! The processing time can vary from embassy to embassy.

Getting your visitor's permit for religious purposes

A visitor's permit for those who want to visit Sweden for more than 90 days (Migrationsverket, 2021j). The validity of the permit you can apply for depends on if you are a missionary or a monk/nun.

If you are a missionary, you can apply for a visitor's permit of up to 1 year. This permit can be extended to a maximum of 3 years, but this is only possible in exceptional cases.

As a monk or nun, you can apply for a visitor's permit that lasts as long as your time at the monastery. However, a maximum of 1-2 years is usually the time initially given. This permit can be extended up to 4 years. At this point, the Swedish Migration Agency can consider granting you a permanent residence permit.

If you're an imam and invited to Sweden to participate in religious activities, these activities are covered by your regular duties. In this case, you need to apply for a work permit instead of a visitor's permit.

It's important to note that if you are granted a visitor's permit for a duration of less than one year, you are not registered as a resident. This means that you need individual medical travel insurance, as you are not entitled to social welfare benefits.

So, what do you need to apply for a visitor's permit for religious purposes? You have to:

- Have a copy of your home country passport, showing personal information and all pages that show entry and exit stamps and visas
- Have a power of attorney if someone else represents you in filling out the application
- Have a certificate from the religious organization, which includes the visit's purpose and the expected length of the visit
- If you have a valid residence permit in another Schengen country, you need a copy of it
- Include an appendix that is filled out by the sponsor who will be responsible for your support during the visit, if you have such a sponsor
- Include a copy of the sponsor's ID card, if you have a sponsor
- Have a passport which is valid for at least 3 months after the end date of your visit
- Be able to support yourself during your time in Sweden
- Have a return ticket or money to buy one

How to apply?

So, how do you apply? How you can send in your application depends on where you are. One option is to use the e-service (Migrationsverket, 2021j). This is, however, only possible in two locations. The first is if you are in Sweden and want to extend your visa. The second is if you are a citizen or permanent resident of Thailand, Myanmar, the Philippines,

Malaysia, Cambodia, Laos, or Taiwan and are submitting your application at the Embassy of Sweden in Bangkok, Thailand.

If you are not in one of these two quite specific situations, you can unfortunately not use the e-service. But not to fret! Instead, you will submit your application at your Swedish embassy or consulate-general. You'll have to fill out form number 165011, which you can download from the Migration Agency's website. As you turn in your application, you will attend an interview to answer some questions about your visit.

Summary

Sweden is a very secular nation and is ranked among the least religious countries in the world. It's, however, also a very tolerant country, and freedom of religion has been part of Swedish law since 1951.

If you wish to go to Sweden for religious purposes, there are two options. If your stay in Sweden is less than 90 days, you'll apply for a visa to visit Sweden for religious purposes. One of the main requirements will be to have an invitation from a religious assembly or organization. Most people will apply for this type of visa through an external service provider. If there isn't an agreement between your embassy and an external service provider, you can apply directly at the embassy with form number 119031 (Application for Schengen Visa). If you're applying from the Swedish embassy in Seoul, Teheran, or Tokyo, you can also apply through an e-service.

If you're going to Sweden for more than 90 days, you can apply for a visitor's permit for religious purposes. As a missionary, you can apply for a permit of up to 1 year at first. If you are a monk or a nun, a maximum of 1-2 years is initially given. If you happen to be applying from the Swedish embassy in Bangkok or extending your visa from within Sweden, then you can apply through the e-service. Otherwise, most people will apply through their Swedish embassy or consulate-general with form number 165011.

Volunteering or being a trainee in Sweden

Volunteering in Sweden is another exciting way to experience Swedish life. First of all, we'd like to applaud you! Thank you for your willing and self-sacrificing spirit. Levels of participation in volunteering activities are relatively high in Scandinavia, and it's definitely true for Sweden (Qvist et al., 2019)!

Without a doubt, NGO activities in Sweden have a wide range. Whether it's Baltic Sea preservation, researching immunodeficiencies, or sled dog racing promotion, Sweden is a special place to be a volunteer (Go Overseas, n.d.-b). Sweden is especially keen on environmental conservation, with many environmental objectives.

The European Solidarity Corps

One common way of volunteering in Sweden as a youth is through the European Solidarity Corps (ESC). It's the main EU volunteering program providing opportunities for youths. It's built on the now discontinued European Voluntary Service's previous success.

According to the European Solidarity Corps (n.d.-a), you can participate in their volunteering activities if you're between 18 and 30 years old. You also have to be a legal resident in an EU Member State or a legal resident in one of the following countries:

- North Macedonia or Turkey

- Iceland, Liechtenstein, or Norway
- Albania, Bosnia and Herzegovina, Kosovo, Montenegro, or Serbia
- Armenia, Azerbaijan, Belarus, Georgia, Moldova, or Ukraine
- Algeria, Egypt, Israel, Jordan, Lebanon, Libya, Morocco, Palestina, Syria, or Tunisia
- Russian Federation

Most of the opportunities are cross-border volunteering activities. Individual volunteering is full-time and can last from 2 to 12 months (European Solidarity Corps, n.d.-b). You can get unforgettable experiences, and you'd be contributing to the work of an organization that is benefiting the local community.

On a related note, there are also opportunities to be a trainee instead of a volunteer. There are full-time traineeships that can last from 2 to 6 months (European Solidarity Corps, n.d.-c). These traineeships are paid for by the organization providing the traineeship. As a trainee, you can gain work experience and develop skills. At the same time, you will help tackle social challenges or help communities in need.

If you don't qualify to be a volunteer with the ESC, there are, of course, still other options to volunteer in Sweden. No matter what kind of volunteer or trainee you are, you'll have to deal with the visa question. So, let's get into it!

Getting your volunteering visa

Depending on your circumstances, there are quite a few options for getting a visa or residence permit to volunteer or be a trainee in Sweden. As we have covered, EU/EEA residents have a right to residence in Sweden and don't need permission to live and work here. What if you're not an EU/EEA resident?

The first option is a residence permit for volunteers within the framework of the European Solidarity Corps. If you want to volunteer in Sweden outside the scope of the European Solidarity Corps, you can apply for a visa for volunteer work or an internship, or a visitor's permit for volunteers or trainees.

Finally, there are separate rules if you are a trainee through an international exchange or a trainee in connection with higher education. Let's look through these five categories and how you can get your visa!

Residence permit for volunteers

If you're a non-EU citizen but will volunteer within the framework of the European Solidarity Corps, you'll need residence permit for volunteer work (Migrationsverket, 2021k).

You can apply by completing form number 157011, "Application for a residence permit for volunteers within the framework of the European Solidarity Corps". You can download the form from the Migration Agency's website. After that, you hand it in at a Swedish embassy or consulate-general in the country you live or the one closest to the country in which you live. If you can't apply in your own country, you can apply at the embassy or consulate-general closest to your country.

If you need a visa to enter Sweden, you'll also have to be photographed and fingerprinted at a Swedish embassy or consulate-general. If you don't need a visa, you can book an appointment at the Swedish Migration Agency to submit documentation for the residence permit after you've arrived in Sweden.

The requirements to be eligible for this type of permit are as follows. You have to:

- Have an agreement with an organization located in Sweden for your participation in a volunteer program within the scope of the ESC
- Have a passport that is valid for the length of your permit
- Have enough money to support your stay in Sweden and to pay for your return home
- Have or have applied for comprehensive health insurance
- Pay a fee (in most cases)

The organization that is offering you work as a volunteer will have to fulfill the following requirements. According to Migrationsverket (2021l), they have to:

- Be approved by the European Solidarity Corps

- Send an agreement on volunteer program participation to the volunteer, including:
- A description of the program content
- The length of the program
- The working and supervision conditions
- The time for volunteer work
- Information on funds available to cover living expenses and housing costs of the volunteer
- Information on potential training that the volunteer will receive to do the volunteer work

Visa for volunteer work or an internship

Do you need or want to apply for another type of volunteer visa? Then you have two options depending on how long you are going to be in Sweden. If you're going for less than 90 days, you can apply for a visa for volunteer work or an internship. If you're going for more than 90 days, you'll need a visitor's residence permit for a volunteer or trainee.

If you're applying for a visa, remember that you need it before traveling to the Schengen area (Migrationsverket, 2021i). Also, you have to apply no earlier than 6 months before traveling. Another important reminder is that you can only work on this type of visa in exceptional cases.

How do you apply? The most common way is to apply through an external service provider. You can visit the website of your embassy to find out about potential options for that. If you don't wish to apply through an external service provider, you can apply directly at the embassy. You will have to hand in form number 119031 (Application for

Schengen Visa). You can download the form from the Migration Agency's website. If you're applying from Sweden's embassy in Seoul, Teheran, or Tokyo, you can also do so through an e-service.

The requirements to receive the visa are as follows. You have to:

- Have an invitation from the volunteer/internship organization
- Describe the purpose of your visit
- Have a passport that is valid for a minimum of three months after the visa has expired (It also needs at least two empty pages, and it has to have been issued in the last ten years)
- Have enough money to support your stay and your journey home (Sweden requires you to have 450 SEK per day in Sweden, which is around 52 USD or 44 EUR)
- Have individual comprehensive medical travel insurance, which is valid for all Schengen countries and covers costs of at least 30 000 EUR (around 35 600 USD)
- Show that you intend to leave the Schengen area on the last day before your visa expires
- A photo in passport format that is not older than six months

Make sure to find more information on your embassy's website to verify other documents you might need.

Visitor's permit for a volunteer or trainee

Wow! You're going to volunteer in Sweden for more than 90 days! You're clearly very dedicated to your cause. You will need a visitor's residence permit for volunteers or trainees (Migrationsverket, 2021j).

How do you apply? You can submit your application at your Swedish embassy or consulate-general. You'll have to fill out form number 165011, which you can download from the Migration Agency's website. As you turn in your application, you'll attend an interview to answer some questions about your visit.

If you're a citizen or permanent resident of Thailand, Myanmar, the Philippines, Malaysia, Cambodia, Laos, or Taiwan and are applying at the Embassy of Sweden in Bangkok, you can also use the e-service instead.

What are the requirements for this type of residence permit? You have to:

- Have a certificate from a company or organization about the purpose and length of your visit
- Have a passport that is valid for at least three months after the end date of your visit
- Include a copy of relevant pages in your home country passport
- Be able to support yourself during your time in Sweden
- have a return ticket or the money to buy one
- Include a copy if you have a valid residence permit in another Schengen country

- Include a power of attorney if someone represents you in filling out the application
- Include an appendix filled out by your sponsor and a copy of their ID card, if you have a sponsor

Are you under the age of 18? If you're traveling without a guardian, the person representing you in the application has to include three additional documents:

- A birth certificate stating the names of your parents
- Power of attorney for the person who is representing you from at least one of your guardians
- A copy of your guardian's passport

Work permit for traineeship through international exchange

Except for the three options above, there are two situations where special rules apply. These situations are; if you are a trainee through international exchange or a trainee in connection with higher education.

Let's say you have been offered a traineeship in Sweden through an international agreement or international exchange (Migrationsverket, 2021m). For example, it might be an international exchange program within an organization like AIESEC, IAESTE, SACCUSA, or JUF. Or it might be an agreement between countries on training exchanges. Sweden has such agreements with the US and Canada, and the EU has an agreement with China for young managers. In all these scenarios, you will need a work permit.

To apply for a work permit as a trainee, you have to:

- Have a valid passport
- Be 18 years of age
- Have received a written traineeship offer
- Have received an e-mail from your employer with the link to the e-service
- Have copies of relevant pages in your passport
- Pay the application fee by card

Your employer is the one who starts the application process through an e-service on the Migration Agency's website. After receiving an e-mail with a link to the e-service, you can continue with the application. If you need a visa to travel to Sweden, you will also have to visit the Swedish embassy or consulate-general to be photographed and fingerprinted. If you don't need a visa, you'll have to be photographed and fingerprinted once you've arrived in Sweden.

Residence permit for internship for higher education

Let's say you've been offered an internship in Sweden that has ties to your ongoing higher education (Migrationsverket, 2021n). The internship is perhaps at a company, a university, an authority, or an organization. If so, you will need a residence permit for the internship.

To be eligible for a trainee residence permit, you have to:

- Have gotten a higher education degree within two years before applying, or currently be pursuing a program that leads to such a degree
- Have gotten a written internship agreement with the conditions of your internship
- Have a passport that is valid for at least the length of your permit
- Have comprehensive health insurance, or have applied for it (if you're staying in Sweden for one year or less)
- Have money to support yourself during your stay in Sweden and pay for your return trip
- Have received an e-mail from your employer with the link to the e-service
- Have copies of relevant pages of your passport
- Have a certificate for ongoing education or a degree within higher education
- Pay the application fee by card

Your employer will get the application started with the e-service on the Migration Agency's website. You will then receive an e-mail with a link to the e-service, at which point you can continue the application. If you need a visa to enter Sweden, you will have to visit the Swedish embassy or consulate-general to be photographed and fingerprinted. If you don't need a visa, you will need to be photographed and fingerprinted after you have arrived in Sweden.

Summary

Volunteering in Sweden can take many forms since NGO activities have a wide range in Sweden. One common way of volunteering in Sweden as a youth is through the European Solidarity Corps (ESC). To apply, you will have to be between 18 and 30 years old and be a legal resident in an EU Member State or one of the following countries;

North Macedonia, Turkey, Iceland, Liechtenstein, Norway, Albania, Bosnia and Herzegovina, Kosovo, Montenegro, Serbia, Armenia, Azerbaijan, Belarus, Georgia, Moldova, Ukraine, Algeria, Egypt, Israel, Jordan, Lebanon, Libya, Morocco, Palestina, Syria, or Tunisia, or the Russian Federation.

There are also options for going to Sweden as a trainee.

As mentioned, EU/EEA residents have a right to residence in Sweden and don't need permission to live and work there. If you're not an EU/EEA resident, there are five options when it comes to visas or visitor's permits.

If you're a non-EU citizen but will volunteer within the framework of the European Solidarity Corps, you'll need a residence permit for volunteer work. You can apply at your Swedish embassy or consulate-general with form number 157011, "Application for a residence permit for volunteers within the framework of the European Solidarity Corps".

But maybe your volunteer work isn't through the European Solidarity Corps. What then? If you're staying in Sweden for less than 90 days, you'll apply for a visa for volunteer work or an internship. Most people will apply through an external service provider for this visa. Don't forget that you'll need an invitation from the volunteer/internship organization.

If you're staying in Sweden for more than 90 days, you'll need a visitor's residence permit for a volunteer or trainee. You'll apply at your Swedish embassy or consulate-general with form number 165011. If you're applying from Bangkok, you might also be able to use an e-service. One primary requirement is a certificate from the company or organization about the purpose and length of your visit.

Special rules apply if you are a trainee through an international exchange or a trainee in connection with higher education. If you've been offered a traineeship through an international exchange, you'll need to apply for a work permit. Your employer will have to start the application process through an e-service on the Migration Agency's website.

If you've been offered an internship in Sweden that has ties to your ongoing higher education, you'll need a trainee residence permit. Your employer will initiate the application through the e-service on the Migration Agency's website. You'll also need a written internship agreement with the conditions of your internship.

Traveling in Sweden

Maybe you didn't pick up this book because you want to move to Sweden. Maybe, you're just interested in Sweden or want to travel there as a tourist? Or perhaps you do want to move to Sweden, but not before you've had the chance to scope out the country and get a feel for your new future home. Then, this section is for you.

When to travel to Sweden?

Sweden is, without a doubt, a place where you can experience all four seasons. Most people want to travel to Sweden in the summer. There's an obvious reason for this. Summer in Sweden means comfortably warm but not overly hot weather and long days. It's the time when Sweden comes alive, and a spirit of festivity often goes hand in hand with the season. However, this also means that the cities have quite an influx of tourists! Something to look out for is the biggest party of the year, Swedish Midsummer, which takes place at the end of June. Summer is a beautiful time to enjoy the cities of Sweden and the never-ending and gorgeous great outdoors. The downside is that summer is the time of prolonged application times, as many people are on summer vacation.

Spring and fall will naturally have cooler temperatures than the summer. Spring lets you enjoy the sight of nature coming alive again after the cold Swedish winter. At the same time, the changing leaves of fall set everything on fire with its beautiful, bright colors. Spring and fall are also great times to explore Sweden, but be sure to bring a jacket. A classic

Swedish saying is: "There is no such thing as bad weather, only bad clothes."

The low season is Swedish winter, which you might have guessed, is cold and dark. However, most will admit that Sweden covered in snow is a beautiful sight. Swedes have had a lot of training in how to survive the colder months. Cities often appear magical, with cozy places to escape the cold at every corner. It's a perfect time to sneak into warm and toasty cafés and have a *"fika"*. If you missed it, *fika* is to Swedes what afternoon tea is for the Brits. It often involves hot beverages, especially coffee, and delicious desserts, or savory snacks. Winter is also the season when Swedes gear up for winter sports. If you love skiing or have always wanted to try it, ski resorts across the country will be waiting for you during the winter months.

Without a doubt, no matter when you choose to travel to Sweden, all four seasons offer a different and unique experience.

Where to go and what to do?

What are things you just can't miss in Sweden? It's a tricky question to answer. The options are numerous. If you are interested in city life, Stockholm is probably what comes to mind first. And the capital does have quite a lot to offer. This includes everything from getting lost in the narrow alleys of the Old Town, island hopping around Stockholm Archipelago, and visiting the Vasa Museum to see the Vasa ship – the greatest preserved failure in history.

However, there are definitely other cities worth visiting in Sweden. Gothenburg is Sweden's second-largest city but has a great laid-back vibe and a slower tempo of life. It's also home to Liseberg, the biggest amusement park in Scandinavia. Other cities you might want to explore are Uppsala with its university or Malmö and the vibrant nightlife.

If you're into history, you can't miss the island Gotland. Gotland's main town is Visby, which is a beautiful walled medieval city. It's also home to beautiful beaches and stalagmite caves.

Of course, the colder part of the year also offers opportunities for winter sports and exploring the frozen lands in the north. You can go skiing at the ski resort Åre, Northern Europe's most prominent sports resort (Visit Sweden, 2020). Other popular winter activities include catching a glimpse of the magnificent Northern Lights or staying at the Ice Hotel. In the north, there's also the possibility of learning more about the Sami culture - an indigenous people and one of Sweden's official national minorities.

Getting your tourist visa

Time to really start planning your Sweden trip! What kind of visa will you need as a tourist? It depends on where you are from and how long you want to stay. As we have already covered, residents from EU/EEA countries have a right to residence in Sweden. But even if you're not an EU citizen, there's still a possibility that you don't need a visa if you wish to visit Sweden for less than 90 days.

Citizens from many countries outside the EU do not need a visa to go to Sweden if the stay is 90 days or less. According to the Government Offices of Sweden (2020), here are the countries whose citizens *do* need a visa to enter Sweden:

Afghanistan, Albania, Algeria, Angola, Armenia, Azerbaijan, Bahrain, Bangladesh, Belarus, Belize, Benin, Bhutan, Bolivia, Bosnia-Hercegovina, Botswana, Burkina Faso, Burundi, Cambodia, Cameroon, Cape Verde, Central African Rep., Chad, China (excluding Hongkong and Macao), Comoros, Congo, Dem. Rep., Congo, Rep., Cuba, Djibouti, Dominican Republic, Ecuador, Egypt, Equitorial Guinea, Eritrea, Ethiopia, Fiji, Gabon, Gambia, Georgia, Ghana, Guinea, Guinea-Bissau, Guyana, Haiti, India, Indonesia, Iran, Iraq, Ivory Coast, Jamaica, Jordan, Kazakhstan, Kenya, Korea (North), Kosovo, Kuwait, Kyrgyzstan, Laos, Lebanon, Lesotho, Liberia, Libya, FYROM, Madagascar, Malawi, Maldives, Mali, Mauritania, Moldova, Mongolia, Montenegro, Morocco, Mozambique, Myanmar, Namibia, Nauru, Nepal, Niger, Nigeria, Northern Mariana Islands, Oman, Pakistan, Palestine, Palestine, Papua New Guinea, The Philippines, Qatar, Russia, Rwanda, Sao Tomé & Principe, Saudi Arabia, Senegal, Serbia, Sierra Leone, Somalia, South Africa, South Sudan, Sri Lanka, Sudan, Surinam, Swaziland, Syria, Taiwan, Tajikistan, Tanzania, Thailand, Togo, Tunisia, Turkey, Turkmenistan, Uganda, Ukraine, Uzbekistan, Vietnam, Yemen, Zambia, Zimbabwe

So, if you're a citizen in one of the countries above, you will need a visa to go to Sweden. Let's get into what you need to apply for one.

Tourist visa for less than 90 days

How can you apply for this type of visa? The most common way people apply for a tourist visa is through an external service provider. You can visit the website of your embassy to find out about potential options for external service providers.

You can also apply directly at the embassy. You'll need to hand in form number 119031 (Application for Schengen Visa), which you can download from the Migration Agency's website (Migrationsverket, 2021i). If you're applying from Sweden's embassy in Seoul, Teheran, or Tokyo, you can also apply through an e-service.

The requirements for receiving a tourist visa are as follows. You have to:

- Have a passport that is valid for a minimum of three months after your visa expires, has two or more empty pages, and was issued in the last ten years
- Describe the purpose of your visit to Sweden
- Have enough money to support yourself and for your travel home (Sweden requires you to have 450 SEK per day of stay in Sweden, which is around 52 USD or 44 EUR, and can also be paid by the person inviting you)
- Have individual comprehensive medical travel insurance, which is valid in all Schengen countries and covers at least 30 000 EUR (around 35 600 USD)
- Show your intention to leave the Schengen area on the last day before your visa expires

- Have a photograph in passport format which is not older than six months
- Have the other documents which your embassy may require

Tourist visitor's permit for more than 90 days

Are you hoping to travel around Sweden for longer than 90 days? You must be really excited to discover all the fantastic things Sweden has to offer. If you want to visit Sweden this long, you will need a visitor's permit (Migrationsverket, 2021j).

If you've entered Sweden on a tourist visa, you can turn in an application for another 3 months from within Sweden. In some cases, it's possible to apply for a permit for up to a total of 9 months. An important detail to remember is that you're not registered as a resident in Sweden during this time. You're also not allowed to work in Sweden during this time.

You can submit your application for a visitor's permit at your Swedish embassy or consulate-general. You need to have filled out form number 165011, which you can download from the Migration Agency's website. When you hand in your application, you'll need to attend an interview to answer some questions about your visit.

If you are a citizen/permanent resident of Thailand, Myanmar, the Philippines, Malaysia, Cambodia, Laos, or Taiwan and are applying at the Embassy of Sweden in Bangkok, then you can also use the e-service to apply.

To apply for a tourist visitor's permit, you have to:

- Have a passport that is valid for a minimum of three months after the end date of your visit
- Have a copy of all relevant pages in your home country passport
- Be able to support yourself during your visit in Sweden
- Have a bank statement or other document showing that you have enough money for your time in Sweden (450 SEK per day of stay in Sweden, which is around 52 USD or 44 EUR)
- Have a return ticket or money to buy one
- Have a copy of your residence permit in another Schengen country if you have one
- Append a power of attorney if someone else is representing you in filling out the application
- Include an appendix filled in by your sponsor, if you have a sponsor
- Include a copy of your sponsor's ID card, if you have a sponsor

Are you under the age of 18 and traveling without a guardian? Then the person filling out your application will also need:

- A birth certificate stating your parents' names
- A copy of your guardian's passport
- A power of attorney or a certificate from at least one of your parents for the person who will represent you

Summary

Perhaps you're planning to travel around Sweden before moving there? Not a bad idea. Let's get into some information you might want to know when traveling to Sweden as a tourist!

When is the best time to travel to Sweden? Most people travel to Sweden during the summer, as it is without a doubt the season with the most comfortable weather. But Sweden is truly a place where you can experience all four seasons. Spring and fall have cooler temperatures but their own charm. Nature comes alive again during the beautiful spring, and the world turns orange, yellow, and red during fall. As we're sure you know, the Swedish winter is cold and dark. But it can also mean cozy cafés and fun winter sports. So, no matter when you choose to travel to Sweden, all four seasons offer a different and unique experience.

Where to go, then? The options are numerous. For city life, Stockholm, Gothenburg, and Uppsala are all cool options to check out. For history, you can't miss Gotland with its medieval city Visby. For winter sports, the ski resort Åre is the place to go.

Now, it's time to talk visas! If you plan to visit Sweden for less than 90 days, there's a chance that you don't need a visa. EU/EEA residents won't need it. Many countries outside the EU/EEA can also travel to Sweden without a visa for less than 90 days. Make sure you check our list of countries whose citizens do need a visa to enter Sweden.

If you do need a visa, you will likely apply through an external service provider. You can also apply directly at your embassy with form number 119031 (Application for Schengen Visa). If you're applying from Sweden's embassy in Seoul, Teheran, or Tokyo, you can also apply through an e-service.

If you wish to travel to Sweden for more than 90 days, you'll need a tourist visitor's permit. If you've entered Sweden on a tourist visa, you can turn in an application for another 3 months from within Sweden. You can apply for a visitor's permit at your Swedish embassy or consulate-general with form number 165011. If you are applying from Bangkok, you might also be able to use the e-service.

Moving to a spouse or partner in Sweden

Maybe your desire to move to Sweden is to live with your special someone. One common reason for moving to a new country is getting married or starting a relationship with someone from another country. If this is your case, this section is for you.

Getting a residence permit for a spouse or partner

If you are a citizen of a non-EU country and wish to move to a spouse or partner in Sweden, you can apply for a residence permit. More specifically, a "resi-dence permit to move to a spouse, regis-tered partner or coha-bi-ting partner in Sweden". There are, however, rules and particular circumstances that need to be met. Let's look at who can apply and how to apply for this type of permit.

Who can apply?

According to Migrationsverket (2021o), this residence permit applies to you if you're married to, have entered a registered partnership with, or have been cohabiting with someone in Sweden. The person you wish to move in with in Sweden has to be a Swedish citizen, have a right of permanent residence, have a permanent residence permit, or have a temporary residence permit as a refugee or a person in need of subsidiary protection.

A brief note about cohabiting partners! Cohabiting partners are called sambo in Swedish, and it's a term you'll likely come across quite a lot during your time in Sweden. Sambo isn't just any roommate though, it refers to something quite specific. To count as cohabiting partners or sambo, it's not enough to simply have lived together briefly with a person during, for example, travel. Cohabiting partners are two people who live together in a type of "marriage-like" relationship. To prove this, you could, for example, enclose a copy of your rental contract showing that you have been living together.

If you're married or in a registered partnership, your spouse or partner will have to register this marriage or partnership. They can do so with the Swedish Tax Agency.

What if you're planning to get married to or become cohabiting partners with a resident of Sweden? Is it possible to move to Sweden before you've actually gotten married or moved in with your special someone? It is possible! In this case, you will be required to show that you and your partner in Sweden have a serious relationship and that the relationship was previously established in the country of origin. It should also be clear that you did not have the possibility of getting married or living together in that country.

Another note is that different rules apply if your spouse or partner's residence permit in Sweden is for work or studies.

The Maintenance Requirement

There's one major requirement you may not be aware of for this type of residence permit. The person you wish to move in with in Sweden has to be able to support you both (Migrationsverket, 2021o). They also need to have suitable accommodation where the two of you can live. The home must be of sufficient size and standard. This is called the maintenance requirement.

Your spouse or partner must fulfill these requirements before you apply. This will save you complicated steps and a lot of time. If you submit updated information about this after a decision has already been made, the decision cannot be reconsidered. It would have to be appealed at the Migration Court, which involves long waiting times (Migrationsverket, 2021p).

How to apply?

First of all, if you're applying for the first time, it's essential to know where you can apply from. You can't submit your application for the permit if you are currently in Sweden (Migrationsverket, 2021q). Instead, you have to return to the country where you are currently a permanent resident and apply from there.

The first time you apply for this permit, you will always receive a temporary residence permit (Migrationsverket, 2021r). This temporary permit can last for up to two years at a time. When you have held such a residence permit for at least three years, you might be eligible for a permanent residence permit.

What is the entire process of getting a residence permit to move to a spouse or partner? According to Migrationsverket (2021s), here are the steps you will have to go through:

- Fill out the application form
- Attach documents and pay the fee
- Your spouse or partner answers a questionnaire
- Book and attend an interview
- Wait for the decision

1. Fill out the application form

So, how do you apply? You can apply by making an online application on the Migration Agency's website. The application gives you clear instructions on how to fill out the form and what to enclose. This will make it easier for you to get everything right from the start, making it more likely for you to get a quicker decision!

Some requirements to apply online are as follows. You have to:

- Have a valid e-mail address
- Be able to pay the fee by Visa or Mastercard
- Be able to scan or photocopy documents that will need to be attached
- Be 18 years of age or older (this also has to be true of your spouse or partner)

You can also have your spouse or partner fill in the application for you. If so, you will need to give them power of attorney. They will have to attach a copy of this power of attorney to the application. Your spouse or partner will also have to complete a questionnaire.

What will you need to fill out the application? You'll have to fill out details about yourself and the person you wish to move in with in Sweden. Some of the information you will need about your spouse or partner is:

- Their phone number
- Their address
- Their e-mail address
- Their Swedish personal identity number

You should also write which Swedish embassy or consulate-general you'll visit for your interview. The embassy or consulate-general should be in the country where you're living. Make sure that the embassy or consulate-general you go to deals with migration cases.

Here's another important reminder! Make sure your passport isn't about to expire. You can't obtain a residence permit that lasts past the validity of your passport.

2. Attach documents and pay the fee

The next step is to attach the necessary documents to the application. All documents have to be translated into either Swedish or English by an authorized public translator. You can usually find several options for translators online, but make sure that you confirm that they are actually authorized professionals. The documents also have to be attached as originals. Which documents will you need to enclose?

You will have to attach:

- Copies of relevant pages in your passport, including pages with your personal details, the period of validity, the country of issue, your signature, potential permissions to live in countries other than your country of origin
- A population registration certificate, proof of purchase or tenancy agreement for your accommodation, or other documents proving you have shared accommodation
- A document proving that you have been living together, for example, a bill or tenancy agreement with both your names

If you are expecting a child, a certificate of pregnancy should also be attached. Furthermore, if children under 18 will be moving with you to Sweden, the following should also be attached:

- Copies of all relevant pages in your child's passport
- A birth certificate showing the names of the parents
- A death certificate if the other parent is deceased, or a court decision if you have sole custody
- Adoption papers in case the child is adopted
- A letter of consent from the other parent if this person is not accompanying you to Sweden, including:
  - The name, birth date, and address of the parent giving consent
  - The name and birth date of the child moving to Sweden

- The parent expressing his/her agreement for the child taking up residence in Sweden and being granted a residence permit there
  - The parent's signature and name in clear script related to them giving their consent

Finally, you can pay the application fee. You can do so with a credit card or a debit card. There are rare cases where you don't have to pay the application fee. If so, the application will make that clear. Once the fee has been paid, your application will be off to the Migration Agency!

3. Your spouse or partner answers a questionnaire

When your application has been received, your spouse or partner will be e-mailed specific instructions. These instructions will guide them to how to access a questionnaire which they will have to answer. They must answer it within 14 days! Don't forget to check the junk folder if your spouse or partner can't find the e-mail.

The questionnaire will include questions about your relationship, income, and accommodation. This is where you'll see the importance of fulfilling the maintenance requirement.

4. Book and attend an interview

When the application and questionnaire have been reviewed, the Swedish Migration Agency will send you an e-mail. This e-mail will ask you to book a time for… an interview! How exciting. Things are moving along. You will have to book a time for the interview at your Swedish embassy or consulate-general.

When you go to your appointment, make sure to bring your passport with you. You'll also need to bring the originals of the documents you attached to your application. If you're applying for your child to move with you, don't forget to bring your child! They will also have to attend the interview.

What will you talk about during your interview? The main questions you will have to answer are related to your relationship with the person in Sweden. If you need a visa to enter Sweden, you'll also have to be fingerprinted and photographed at the embassy or the consulate-general. This photo and your fingerprints are for your residence permit card.

5. Wait for the decision

Now it's time to wait for the Migration Agency to make their decision. If they need more information from you, they will contact you. If you need to provide additional information, you do so by e-mail.

While you're waiting for the decision, it's possible to apply for a visa for a temporary visit to Sweden. Typically, though, a residence permit can't be granted while you are in Sweden. So, it's very important that you leave Sweden and return home when your temporary visa expires. You should wait there for the decision on your application.

When the decision has finally been made, you'll get that decision by e-mail. You can then contact your embassy or consulate-general and collect it!

Summary

Maybe you wish to move to Sweden to be with your special someone. You're not alone. Getting married or starting a relationship with someone from another country is a common reason for moving abroad. When it comes to getting a residence permit to move to your partner, some specific rules and circumstances need to be met.

What are the requirements to obtain a "residence permit to move to a spouse, registered partner, or cohabiting partner in Sweden"? First of all, the person you wish to move to has to be a Swedish citizen. They also need to have a right of permanent residence, have a permanent residence permit, or have a temporary residence permit as a refugee or a person in need of subsidiary protection.

In general, you have to be married to, have entered a registered partnership, or cohabitate with someone in Sweden. What about if you're planning to get married to or become cohabiting partners with a Swedish resident? In that case, you will have to show that you have a serious relationship and have not had the possibility of getting married or living together in the country of origin. Cohabiting partners are called sambo in Swedish. To be counted as sambo, you have to have lived together in a type of "marriage-like" relationship.

An important thing to be aware of is the maintenance requirement. Your marriage partner or partner in Sweden has to be able to support you both. They also need to have suitable accommodation where the two of you can live.

How do you apply for this type of residence permit? You will have to apply from the country where you are currently a resident. You cannot apply from Sweden. Here are the five steps you'll have to follow to get a residence permit to move to a spouse or partner:

- Fill out the application form
- Attach documents and pay the fee
- Your spouse or partner answers a questionnaire
- Book and attend an interview
- Wait for the decision

Different rules apply if your spouse or partner's residence permit in Sweden is for work or studies. Make sure to look up the rules for your specific situation.

Where in Sweden do you want to live?

So, you've decided that Sweden is for you. But *where* in Sweden? Let's look at some of the options for different cities and areas you might be interested in living in. If you're moving to Sweden for work or studies, you'll need to know about the living costs, the general lifestyle, and other relevant factors of various places in Sweden.

The cost of living is definitely something to keep in mind when moving to Sweden. You'll need to make sure you can afford the cost of living in Sweden. The cost of living is high, primarily due to the competitive housing market and the high tax rate. It's challenging to state how much money a person will need to live in Swede since it varies considerably based on each person's lifestyle. However, we'll try to give a few average numbers to help you compare different places in Sweden! The average living costs are taken from Livingcost.org (n.d.). Let's see if we can find a place for you.

The capital Stockholm

First of all, we have to talk about Sweden's capital Stockholm! Stockholm is the largest city not only in Sweden but in Scandinavia. If you're a big city person, Stockholm might be the best fit for you. There's a lot going on, and you'll likely find options no matter your interest or hobbies. Needless to say, there's also an endless array of bars, restaurants, and cultural attractions. Stockholm also has a thriving job market and some great universities. Excellent internet is guaranteed by the outstanding fiber-optic network, so no complaints about that either.

At the same time, Stockholm still manages to provide a lifestyle only one step away from nature. The city is built on 14 different islands, meaning you have a lot of access to water and the beautiful views that come with it (British Expat Guide, 2016). In the city, you're seldom far from a good park. And if you head a little further towards the suburbs, you'll find beautiful forests and other charming landscapes.

The most apparent downside to Stockholm is, however, the cost of living. The cost of renting accommodation can be a shock in itself. Stockholm is, unfortunately, one of Europe's most expensive cities when it comes to renting a place to stay. The average cost of living for one person in Sweden is approximately 1 871 USD (1 577 EUR). The average cost of living for a family of 4 is around 3 936 USD (3 318 EUR).

As a small note, and in connection with Stockholm, we'd also like to mention Solna. Solna is a beautiful city just north of Stockholm which routinely gets voted as one of the best cities in Sweden. It's just on Stockholm's doorstep and has an impressive job market. At the same time, it allows for a slightly quieter and more suburban way of life. Stockholm is, however, far from your last option if you're considering cities in Sweden.

Sweden's second-largest city Gothenburg

Heading to the Swedish west coast, you'll find Sweden's second-largest city Gothenburg. It's an excellent option for people who still want an urban lifestyle but with a slightly more laid-back vibe than the capital.

Gothenburg also has an excellent eco-friendly public transport network which makes it easy to get around the city. With the transport pass, you can ride trains, buses, trams, and even ferries to nearby islands. Gothenburg has a diverse population and a great array of cultural events. It's also home to the largest film festival in Scandinavia (British Expat Guide, 2016).

The average cost of living is a bit cheaper than in Stockholm, at 1 566 USD (1 320 EUR) for one person and 3 446 USD (2 905 EUR) for a family of four.

Sweden's southern city Malmö

Going even further south, you'll get to the third-largest city in Sweden – Malmö. It's one of the most diverse cities in Sweden, and they have accepted many refugees. It's renowned for being a very welcoming city for people interested in moving there for work or studies. Malmö is a hub for tech companies, startups, and students. It is viewed by some as a younger and hipper alternative compared to Stockholm.

A little bonus is that the city is connected by bridge to the Danish capital Copenhagen. In 30-45 minutes, you can find yourself exploring another Scandinavian country for the afternoon (Nomad Guide, 2021)!

Malmö is also more affordable than our previous two options. The average cost of living for one person is approximately 1 430 USD (1 206 EUR). The cost of living for a family of four is around 3 267 USD (2 754 EUR).

The best student cities in Sweden

If you're thinking about moving to Sweden for studies, you're likely interested in the student cities of Sweden. Stockholm, Gothenburg, and Malmö are all popular options for students. Still, other cities in Sweden present truly great choices too.

First of all, we have to mention Uppsala, a city known for its university and student culture. Uppsala University is well-reputed and is the oldest Swedish university still in existence, dating back to 1477 (Study.eu, n.d.-b). Uppsala is also the country's fourth-largest city, where more than a quarter of its residents are students. Another benefit of Uppsala is that it's only 40 minutes by train from Stockholm. The average cost of living is 1 403 USD (1 183 EUR) for one person and 3 098 USD (2 612 EUR) for a family of four.

Another famous student city in Sweden is Lund, a smaller city neighboring Malmö. Almost half of its 90 000 citizens are students at the large Lund University (Stimac, 2020). At Lund University, you have over 300 university programs and 2 000 courses to choose from. The average cost of living is 1 471 USD (1 240 EUR) for one person and 3 683 USD (3 105 EUR) for a family of four.

Umeå is definitely the most northern city we've mentioned here so far, only 400 km from the Arctic Circle. Umeå has a distinct university town vibe with its two universities bringing in nearly 39 000 students every academic year. If you're hoping to explore the north of Sweden and maybe spot the

Northern Lights during your stay in Sweden, this is a perfect option – if you're brave enough. Umeå is also comparatively more affordable than the previous cities we've looked at. The average cost of living is 1 227 USD (1 034 EUR) for one person and 2 804 USD (2 364 EUR) for a family of four.

Many other Swedish student cities could be mentioned, so don't forget to keep researching if you want to know about even more options!

Experiencing the Swedish countryside

If the living costs of Swedish cities scare you, you're not alone. One option more and more people consider is moving to the countryside. Rural Sweden can be an attractive place to live but also presents its own challenges. Some popular rural areas are found around Gävle, Skellefteå, Norrtälje, Hofors and Boden.

One great advantage of living in rural Sweden will be living close to nature, for example, the coast or ski slopes. If you want to have a large garden or the great outdoors just outside your doorsteps, this is where to go.

Another good reason to move to the Swedish countryside is if you are interested in genuinely settling down in Sweden and want to buy a house. Buying a home in rural areas will be significantly cheaper than in the cities. So, if you're up for living a calmer lifestyle, the price of housing is definitely a plus.

Now to the downsides. Naturally, finding a well-paying job in the Swedish countryside might be a challenge. It can be even more challenging for foreigners even though the government has initiated a program to promote entrepreneurship and growth in these areas.

Another potential downside is the lack of entertainment. Rural areas will naturally not have the same array of bars, clubs, or malls. However, small local stores and pharmacies should provide all the bare essentials you'll need. What these areas might lack in upscale clubs, they make up for with outdoor activities. Replace your window shopping with hiking, swimming, fishing, or skiing!

When it comes to transportation, there will generally be a few bus services connecting rural areas to major cities and towns. Many people settling in these areas will, however, get around in private cars.

Settling down in northern Sweden

Northern Sweden, or Norrland as Swedes call it, covers over 60% of the country's total area. It's also the least populated area in the country. Naturally, that means that there's a lot of countryside in northern Sweden, which you've just read a bit about it in our countryside section. Like the rural areas of Sweden, Norrland brings a mystical natural beauty and a few challenges.

As northern Sweden is such a large area, it's hard to sum up all the variations of this massive area without generalizing. However, many of the benefits and challenges of the region remain the same. One big challenge is the weather. While summers can be beautiful, they are pretty short, and the year is still dominated by the many winter months. Temperatures can vary over the large area, but suffice to say, it can get very cold and dark. Up in Kiruna, just north of the Arctic circle, the temperature can drop to -40°C (-40 °F) during the worst cold spells (Climate to Travel, n.d.).

The more positive sides to northern Sweden are similar to the pros mentioned about the Swedish countryside. Housing prices are often lower, and the magical natural landscapes will amaze you. It's a calmer but colder lifestyle. It can be a lovely place to live with the right clothes and a good attitude.

Summary

Which Swedish region is right for you? Let's quickly summarize some exciting options.

Stockholm is the capital of Sweden and the largest city in Scandinavia. If you like big cities, this might be the best fit for you! However, Stockholm is also one of Europe's most expensive cities when it comes to accommodation. The average cost of living for one person in Sweden is approximately 1 871 USD (1 577 EUR).

Gothenburg is Sweden's second-largest city and has a more laid-back vibe. The average cost of living is 1 566 USD (1 320 EUR) for one person.

Malmö is the third-largest city in Sweden and is one of the most diverse cities in Sweden. Malmö is a hub for tech companies, startups, and students. The average cost of living for one person is approximately 1 430 USD (1 206 EUR).

Then we have the student cities of Sweden. Uppsala is known for its well-reputed Uppsala university and its student culture. The average cost of living is 1 403 USD (1 183 EUR) for one person. Lund is a smaller city neighboring Malmö in southern Sweden. Almost half of its 90 000 citizens are students at Lund University. The average cost of living is 1 471 USD (1 240 EUR) for one person. On the other side of the country, the city Umeå is only 400 km from the Arctic Circle. Its two universities bring in nearly 39 000 students every academic year. The average cost of living is 1 227 USD (1 034 EUR) for one person.

More and more people consider moving to the countryside, where living costs can be lower than in the cities. Buying a home in rural areas will be significantly cheaper than in the cities. Another great advantage of living in rural Sweden is the closeness to nature. However, there are also downsides. Finding a well-paying job in the Swedish countryside can be a challenge. Naturally, the countryside will also not have as many bars, malls, and the like.

Northern Sweden covers over 60% of the country's total area, but it's the least populated area. The big challenge will be the weather, as winter dominates the year. However, it offers magical natural landscapes and lower housing prices.

Finding the right type of accommodation

When you've decided where in Sweden to settle, it's time to find your new home. Whether you're planning on staying in a dorm, renting a place, or buying a property, finding the right place is an important step.

Unfortunately, finding housing in Sweden is usually described as a bit of a nightmare. It's generally regarded as much more complicated than it is in other European countries. This is especially the case when it comes to renting a place. This is because of the lack of housing in the country. So yes, finding the right home might require a little patience. But it's, of course, not impossible. To help you along the way, we'll try to give you the information you need. Let's start with renting!

Renting an apartment or house

Because of the housing shortage, renting a house or an apartment in Sweden is quite competitive. There is even a black market for long-term leases. The actual process of renting a place is not difficult, but the challenge will be actually finding a place. This is especially the case in the city center.

The good news is that the quality of the housing you'll eventually find is generally going to be very good. No matter where in Sweden you go, there will often be many different options of accommodation. For example, there will be different types of apartments and houses and both furnished and unfurnished places.

The next con is that the price of rent is usually relatively high. On average, rent usually consumes about 30% of a resident's salary.

When looking for rentals in Sweden, you will quickly come across two essential terms. They are "first-hand" and "second-hand" rentals. First-hand rentals are rented directly through a landlord, while second-hand rentals are sublet through the current tenant.

First-hand rentals

Most people hope to find a first-hand contract and rent a place directly through the landlord. These rentals are, however, very limited. Unless you are incredibly fortunate, you will likely live in quite a few second-hand rentals before finally getting a first-hand contract. In popular areas, you might have to wait for several years on the waiting list before you get a first-hand rental.

To be eligible for a first-hand contract, you'll need the following (InterNations GO!, 2020a):

- Proof of sufficient income
- A *personnummer* (a Swedish ID number)
- An employment contract

If the landlord feels that your income is too low, they might also require a guarantor.

Second-hand rentals

As first-hand rentals are limited, subletting a second-hand rental is often the only option when you first arrive in Sweden. Something to be aware of is that these second-hand contracts are sometimes only for a few months or a year. You might therefore find yourself moving fairly frequently during your first few years in Sweden.

People tend to prefer first-hand contracts because second-hand leases are typically more expensive. There has been a phenomenon of landlords overcharging second-hand leases by a significant amount because they're aware of the high demand of finding accommodation.

To be eligible for a second-hand contract, you'll need to provide documents and fulfill requirements that are similar to a first-hand contract, which requires (InterNations GO!, 2020a):

- Proof of sufficient income
- A *personnummer* (a Swedish ID number)
- An employment contract

Another thing to keep in mind is to ensure that the original landlord approves second-hand leasing. Some landlords do not allow subletting, so make sure that this is not the case.

Renting a place through Airbnb

If you're coming to Sweden for a shorter period of time, you might just be looking for a temporary rental. One popular option internationally for short-term rentals is Airbnb.

Considering Sweden's complex housing market, Airbnb was at first questioned. Some housing companies were reluctant to allow it, and there was a landmark case where a woman in Stockholm was banned from renting out her place on the site (Routes North, n.d.-a).

But you'll be happy to know that Airbnb is legal in Sweden. The site provides many options for both accommodation and experiences in the country.

Student accommodation

If you're coming to Sweden as a student, you might be interested in student accommodation. As a first step, we would absolutely recommend checking with your university. Some universities will provide guaranteed housing for their international students. Others may not but can usually offer some kind of accommodation service.

Student accommodation is often cheaper and easier to find than other rentals in Sweden. It's also generally quite different from the dorm life you might encounter in, for example, the US. Two common types of student accommodation in Sweden are corridor rooms and student apartments (Study in Sweden, n.d.-b).

A corridor room will be in a student residence hall. Every corridor might have 10-15 single rooms, a shared kitchen, and common room. Some corridors might also have shared facilities, while others include a bathroom in each corridor room.

A student apartment might have two to four single bedrooms, with a shared bathroom, kitchen, and common room. A benefit of both student apartments and corridor rooms is that you have your own space. At the same time, you have many opportunities to hang out with other international students in common areas.

If sharing is not your thing, finding a studio apartment with a kitchen and bathroom in one unit can also be possible.

Buying a property

As the rental market in Sweden is so challenging, many who want to stay long-term in Sweden will look into the possibility of buying a home. Considering the moving and rental fees involved with moving from one second-hand rental to the next, it's a decision that many make. Another encouraging factor is that Sweden boasts relatively low interest rates.

When looking into buying a house, you might stumble across some Swedish words to describe certain types of properties. Here are a few common types:

- *Lägenhet*: Apartment
- *Fritidshus*: Vacation house
- *Radhus*:   Row house
- *Kedjehus*: Terraced house
- *Villa*: Single-family house

Note that *villa* refers to something entirely different than the mansion-like estate we might envision when we hear the word "villa". A Swedish *villa* is simply a single-family detached home.

If you buy a home in Sweden with a mortgage, you will need a few things to secure the mortgage (InterNations GO!, 2020a). You need:

- A *personnummer* (Swedish ID number)
- A Swedish ID card
- A residency permit
- Proof of employment and a steady income
- Credit history

What are the steps for buying a home?

Searching for a home: You can search for properties on real estate and property platforms. Some popular ones in Sweden include Hemnet, Boneo, Bovision and Booli.

- Bidding: When you've found a place you like, you place a bid on it. You might find yourself in a bidding war.
- Negotiating and surveying: If your bid is accepted, you'll have to negotiate a purchase agreement. During negotiations, you should also hire surveyors to inspect to property. If you feel unable to do so, the real estate agency might be able to help with this.
- Signing: The real estate agent will draft and validate a contract, and you and the seller can then sign the contract.
- Paying the down payment: The down payment can vary, but it's around 10% on average.
- Final signing: You will now receive the keys, sign a contract of sale, and work out mortgage details. The bank or real estate agent will send your final contract. Within a

few weeks, you'll receive verification that the property is officially yours!

It's also wise to be aware of some of the extra fees you might have to pay in connection with buying your property. Except for the mortgage and deposit, you'll also have to pay for the survey of the property. You'll also need to pay for the title deed and the mortgage deed.

The price of the transfer survey (överlåtelsebesiktning in Swedish) of the property is generally around 7 000 – 16 000 SEK. That corresponds to approximately 797 – 1822 USD or 689 – 1574 EUR (The Local, 2020).

Another cost is the title deed (lagfart in Swedish), which is the proof of ownership. Within three months of completing your purchase, you must register your ownership with the Swedish Land Registry. The cost of this will include stamp duty (around 1,5% of purchase price) and a fee of about 825 SEK (94 USD or 81 EUR).

Finally, you'll have to pay a mortgage deed (pantbrev in Swedish). This is basically the bank's proof of security. The cost of a new mortgage deed is 2% of the amount of the mortgage deed. There's also a fee of around 375 SEK (43 USD or 37 EUR). For example, if you need to take out a loan of 1 000 000 SEK, you will pay 20 375 SEK (0,02 * 1 000 000 + 375).

Make sure to also research the prices of utility fees in the area and find out what applies to you regarding annual property tax. It's crucial to be able to expect those "unexpected" fees!

Can buying a house secure permanent residency or citizenship? Unfortunately, not. First of all, buying a property doesn't secure you a residency permit because you need a permit before buying a home. Requirements to receive permanent residency or citizenship are more related to the time you've lived in Sweden than anything else.

Summary

Time to find your new home! Whether you're planning on staying in a dorm, renting a place, or buying a property, finding housing is usually described as a bit of a nightmare. This is because of the housing shortage in Sweden. But, nothing is impossible with some patience and effort.

Renting a house or apartment in Sweden is quite competitive. The price is unfortunately also relatively high, with rent usually consuming about 30% of salaries. You will need to know two essential terms. They are "first-hand" and "second-hand" rentals. First-hand rentals are rented directly through a landlord, while second-hand rentals are sublet through the current tenant.

First-hand rentals are limited, and you might have to wait several years before you get one. This means you will likely be staying in a second-hand rental for a few years. To be eligible for a contract, you will need the following:

- proof of sufficient income
- a *personnummer* (a Swedish ID number
- an employment contract

Maybe you're looking for a more temporary solution? You'll be happy to know that Airbnb is an option. The site provides many options for both accommodation and experiences in the country.

If you're coming to Sweden as a student, we recommend asking your university first about student accommodation. Some universities will provide guaranteed housing for their international students. Two common types of student accommodation in Sweden are corridor rooms and student apartments.

Perhaps you are looking to buy your own home in Sweden. Here are the 6 steps for buying a home in Sweden:

- Searching for a home
- Bidding
- Negotiating and surveying
- Signing
- Paying the down payment
- Final signing

Make sure to be aware of the extra fees of buying a home, such as the fees for the transfer survey, the title deed, and the mortgage deed.

What to think about before you depart

Are you ready? If you've arrived at this section, you're probably quite close to finally leaving for Sweden! Let's look at a few final things you might want to think about before leaving for Sweden.

Packing

When packing, you'll want to consider what you might need to bring, but also what you might need to know regarding shipping and customs. Let's start with what you should pack.

What to pack?

When it comes to packing, the first thing that might come to mind is warm clothes. That's not a bad instinct! Keep Sweden's climate in mind and look up the temperatures and weather of the city or area in Sweden where you're going.

Dress for the weather

If you're going for more than a year, remember that the weather varies significantly between the four seasons. You'll need very warm clothes for the winter, including hats, gloves, and scarves. For the summer, you'll also need clothes for warmer weather, but remember to bring thinner jackets and warmer layers as well. No matter the season, Swedes will recommend you to take lots of layers with you. Dressing in layers upon layers (*lager på lager* in Swedish) is something

Swedes live by, and there's a good reason for that. The weather can vary a lot in Sweden, even during one day. If you're wearing several thinner layers, you'll be able to take off and put on the right number of layers to fit the current weather.

Electronics and outlets

Another thing to keep in mind is electronics. Sweden uses the standard European Type F sockets. Depending on where in the world you're from, you might need to bring adapters. That way, you'll still be able to charge and use your electronic devices when you're in Sweden. However, you should also keep the voltage in mind!

For example, the voltage is often 220 – 240 V in Europe and 100 – 127 V in the US. If you plug in a low voltage item into a high voltage socket, your device might be destroyed. If your device is the wrong voltage, you might also have to look into potential adapters or the possibility of buying a new device in Sweden. Some people also find that smartphone batteries die faster in the cold Swedish weather. In such cases, bringing a portable phone charger is not a bad idea.

Miscellaneous

Apart from clothes and adapters, there are many other things you will need to bring, such as important documents and cards, comfortable footwear, rain gear, toiletries, a medicine bag, and so on. Exactly what you need depends on how long you're going for and your personal circumstances.

But we'd recommend not wasting your luggage space on things like deodorant, shampoo, toothpaste, and other necessities. Don't worry, we have plenty of those things in Sweden too. You'll be able to find a variety of different brands, local and international, in Swedish supermarkets.

When it comes to books, you will find a selection of English books in most Swedish bookstores and libraries. However, if you want to read books in your native language, it might be a good idea to bring a few with you. Another option would be Kindle or other e-book readers so that you can bring your whole library in one device.

If you're moving to Sweden and planning to settle there, you might be bringing quite a lot of your things. If that's the case, it might be good to be aware of methods to get your stuff over to Sweden!

Moving your stuff to Sweden

When you're done with packing, it's almost time to start moving. Perhaps you're heading to Sweden with only the bags you're bringing on the plane. Good for you, minimalist! But if not, you might need some options on actually getting your things over to Sweden.

Shipping your items via a cargo ship can be one of the cheapest options but will take the longest time. Shipping your things via water transport can also take up to several months, depending on where you currently live.

The more popular methods are air transport and ground transport. These forms of transportation are more expensive but far more efficient. It's a classic decision you have to make: Quick and costly or slow and cheap?

When it comes to customs, EU/EEA citizens can bring most household goods with them without declaring it at the Swedish border (InterNations GO!, 2020b). If you're not an EU/EEA citizen, you'll need to fill out a customs form. As long as you can provide proof that your household items are not for commercial sale, it's usually not a problem.

When you present or claim your goods at customs, you'll need:

- A valid passport
- A detailed itemized list of the items
- A completed Swedish custom form

It's also good to be aware of custom allowances in Sweden. Some items are prohibited from being imported to Sweden, such as ammunition and firearms, unprescribed narcotics and medicine, and meat or dairy products from outside the EU/EEA.

If you're a non-EU/EEA citizen, there are also the following limits on certain items:

- One liter of spirits above 22% ABV
- Two liters of spirits below 22% ABV
- 16 liters of beer
- Four liters of wine
- 250 grams of tobacco
- 200 cigarettes

- 100 cigarillos
- 50 cigars
- Other goods valued up to 4 300 SEK (501 USD or 423 EUR)

After you've decided what to bring, don't forget to plan what you'll do with the rest of your things! If you're moving to Sweden for a long time or for good, there might be things you want to get rid of. Perhaps you're planning to dump off boxes of memorabilia at your parent's house. Maybe you can sell some things and earn extra money for your big move. Whatever your method, make sure you have a place for your items.

Health insurance

Before going to Sweden, you'll definitely want to check if you're covered. We're talking about health insurance. This is something you'll want to make sure to figure out before your trip.

If you're from an EU/EEA country, you should register for a European Health Insurance Card (or EHIC for short). This card will grant you the same healthcare access that Swedish citizens get at the same prices (Wise, 2017).

What if you're not an EU/EEA citizen? Then, your situation might depend on how long you're staying in Sweden. Are you getting a residence permit for over a year and will receive a Swedish ID number (*personnummer*)? Great, that *personnummer* will give you healthcare access. However, it might take some time to get this ID number after you arrive in Sweden. It is therefore essential that you have private insurance until you receive this number.

If your visa or permit is for less than one year, you won't be receiving a Swedish ID number. This means that you'll have to take care of your own insurance. You can get private insurance from your country or a private provider. You can also get comprehensive travel insurance for the duration of your stay in Sweden.

It's not illegal to not have health insurance in Sweden, but there is the risk of paying large medical bills if something happens. Make sure you have health insurance, so you don't have to deal with unpleasant surprises.

On the subject of health, we'd also like to briefly mention some vaccinations and health requirements for Sweden (InterNations GO!, 2020b). Moving to Sweden, you are expected to have been vaccinated against:

- Chickenpox
- Diphtheria-tetanus-pertussis
- Measles-mumps-rubella
- Polio vaccine

It is also recommended to be vaccinated against:

- Hepatitis A & B
- Meningitis
- Pneumonia
- Rabies
- Shingles

Sweden also recommends that people get vaccinated against tick-borne encephalitis (TBE) before arriving in Sweden. This might be especially important for those who plan to spend a lot of time in Sweden's beautiful nature.

It's worth mentioning that this book is being published at a time when the COVID-19 pandemic is still putting a lot of restrictions on travel. It's still unclear what requirements will be put in place in the future regarding vaccinations and tests. Always look up the most recent information before any travels to or from Sweden.

Bringing your pet with you

If you're a pet owner, we're sure you've considered how to bring your beloved pet with you. Can you bring your pet with you? Most likely, yes! You will, however, need to make sure that your pet meets the EU animal import requirements. These requirements can vary depending on where you come from, so make sure to look up the rules that apply to your country (InterNations GO!, 2020b).

Here are some basic requirements for bringing your cat, dog, or ferret into Sweden. Your pet has to:

- Have been vaccinated against rabies, no less than 21 days before arriving in Sweden
- Have proof of that vaccination
- Have been microchipped
- Have an EU passport or a valid veterinary certificate
- Have an owner's declaration for pets
- Arrive in Sweden within five days of your arrival

So, when you apply, you will need a form stating that the animal is yours and a veterinary certificate. Apart from this, you'll also have to include a copy of your travel documents.

What about other pets? It's possible to bring reptiles and many other animals with you as well. The requirement for reptiles and certain other animals is to provide proof that the animal was born and raised in captivity. The pet will also have to be transported with the owner.

If you're importing a horse, the horse needs to be examined by a vet 48 hours before arrival in Sweden. Your horse will need a health certificate signed by the vet, stating that the animal is healthy according to EU standards. It's also good to know that you'll have to carry this certificate with you for six months.

After you've made sure of the requirements, you'll have to look into how to actually transport your pet. Pets are often transported in planes as live animal cargo. That means that your pet will be in a special compartment in the plane's hold, which is heated and pressurized (Experts for Expats, 2017). Animals can sometimes also be brought as carry-on baggage. However, specific requirements regarding the weight and size of the animal and pet carrier must be met. Each airline has different requirements, so make sure to communicate with the airline and find out their specific rules.

In most cases, you'll bring your pet through a specialist animal transfer company. They'll take care of the process for you and ensure that your pet is properly looked after during transportation. It's a good idea to research several animal transfer companies and get quotes before making your decision. This will likely be a pretty stressful experience for your pet, so make sure that you let them bring their favorite blanket or toy on the ride!

Utilities

Another thing to keep in mind is making sure you've tied up loose ends at home when it comes to utilities. You might want to contact some utility providers and let them know you will be moving and, if possible, tell them your new address. This can be tricky if you don't have an address yet. Some options can be to temporarily use a family member's address or get a virtual address.

If you are moving out, you will also have to advise your landlord. Make sure to find out how many weeks or months in advance you have to give notice before leaving. Moving out can be stressful, so, if possible, try not to move out the day you leave for Sweden. Look into the possibility of staying with family or friends for a few days, to make sure things with your old place are settled.

If you're keeping your place in your home country, you might want to contact your providers of electricity, gas, water, and broadband and let them know that you're moving. This will make sure you avoid unnecessary fees. You may also want to contact your private pension providers and your bank to let them know you're moving abroad.

Bank and taxes

It's essential to contact your bank to let them know you will be abroad. If you don't, there's a risk that they'll block your cards. You might also want to check your bank's charges before going. Many banks levy charges for both debit and credit card transactions abroad (Routes North, n.d.-b). Before you get a Swedish bank account, you'll likely have to use your foreign card a lot. Checking your bank's charges for withdrawing or transferring cash helps you avoid unpleasant surprises when you arrive.

Don't forget that you might also have to notify the tax authorities in your home country that you are moving. If you're moving to Sweden for work, you might be exempt from certain taxes in your home country (Experts for Expats, 2021). You'll likely be taxed in Sweden soon. If you don't make sure that your tax authorities know that you're leaving, you might end up having your income taxed twice! Why pay more taxes than you have to, right?

Subscriptions and phone plans

You might also want to cancel certain subscriptions, such as cable TV or a gym membership. You likely will also cancel your current phone plan. When it comes to your cell phone, you might also want to make sure it's unlocked. What does that mean?

If you plan on using your cell phone in Sweden, you'll likely get a new SIM card in Sweden to put in your phone. Certain cell phones are, however, "locked" to a specific carrier. To put it simply, you can't put a new Swedish SIM card in a locked phone. If you're unsure if your phone is locked or not, contact your carrier. If your phone is locked, you can ask them about the possibilities of "unlocking" it.

Summary

If you've arrived at this section, you're probably quite close to finally leaving for Sweden! One question that might hit you is: What will I need to pack? First of all, you'll have to consider the weather. Sweden has four seasons, and you'll need appropriate clothes for all of them. We recommend many thinner pieces of clothing that can be layered on top of each other. That's the Swedish way. When it comes to the winter, don't forget a hat, gloves, and scarves.

When it comes to electronics, you might need to bring adapters. Sweden uses the standard European Type F sockets. The voltage is often 220 – 240 V. When it comes to packing the rest of your belonging, precisely what you need depends on how long you're going for and your personal circumstances.

If you're moving to Sweden with a lot of things, you might want to consider shipping your items. Shipping via a cargo ship can be a cheap option but will take the longest time. Air transport and ground transport are more expensive but also more efficient. Something else to be aware of: if you are a non-EU/EEA resident, you'll have to fill out a customs form.

What about health insurance? EU/EEA residents should register for a European Health Insurance Card (EHIC). What if you're a non-EU/EEA resident? If you're getting a residence permit and will receive a Swedish ID number (*personummer*), that number will get you health care access in Sweden. Just make sure you have insurance that covers you until you get that number. If you aren't getting a Swedish ID number, you must ensure you're covered by your own private insurance during your stay in Sweden. And don't forget to check our list of recommended vaccinations before departure!

If you plan on bringing your pet with you, you'll need to make sure that your pet meets the EU animal import requirements. Pets are often transported in planes as live animal cargo. Animals can sometimes also be brought along as carry-on baggage. In most cases, you'll bring your pet through a specialist animal transfer company.

Make sure you tie up loose ends at home when it comes to utilities. Let your utility providers know that you're moving. You should also advise your landlord in advance if you're moving out.

It's also important to let your bank know that you're moving abroad. If you don't, there's a risk that they'll block your cards. You might also have to notify the tax authorities in your home country that you are moving.

And don't forget to cancel any subscriptions and your phone plan. When it comes to your cell phone, you might also want to make sure it's unlocked.

What to think about when arriving in Sweden?

The day has finally come! You're in Sweden! You're probably super excited and maybe a little nervous. Try to enjoy the moment. But there are indeed a few things you'll have to start thinking about.

Remember, you're allowed to ask for help! Don't be afraid to ask questions, and save a few valuable numbers you can call when you need answers. For example, you might want to look up the number of your local embassy in Sweden if you have questions that they might be able to help you with. While you're at it, make sure to make a note of other useful numbers to have in Sweden. For example:

- Emergencies (police, ambulance, and fire department): 112
- Medical advice: 1177
- Police for non-emergency incidents: 11414
- Information about non-emergency accidents and emergencies: 11313

Now, back to your first day in Sweden. You might be thinking about all the things you have to do. When can you go register with the Tax Agency? When can you open a Swedish bank account? One step at a time! We'll try to guide you through the things you'll have to take care of after you've arrived in Sweden.

The Swedish Migration Agency

First of all, you'll need your residence permit. If you haven't yet received your residence permit, it's time now. After arriving in Sweden, it's recommended to book an appointment at Migrationsverket, the Swedish Migration Agency, as soon as possible.

At the Migration Agency, you'll have your fingerprints and your picture taken. Don't forget to bring your passport to the appointment! An order will be made for your residence permit card. And it will be sent to your address in Sweden when it's ready (Migrationsverket, 2021t).

If you have an entry visa for Sweden, you might already have been photographed and fingerprinted at your embassy and received your residence permit. It can still be a good idea to locate your nearest Migration Agency office. This way, you'll know where it is, if there are any issues or if you need to renew any permits.

The Swedish Tax Agency

As a new resident in Sweden, a vital step is also to register with the Swedish Tax Agency (Skatteverket). This registration process is called *folkbokföring* in Swedish. The process adds you to the system for tax collection, personal identification, mailing address information, insurance purposes, and marital status monitoring (Sweden.se, 2021d).

When you've registered, you will receive your *personnummer*. This is the personal identification number or Swedish ID number. Your legal identity in Sweden hinges on this number. It truly is an access key to many services in Sweden, and your life will be made much easier once you've received this magic number.

Once you have your Swedish ID number, a good next step is to get a Swedish ID card! To apply for an ID card, you'll have to make another appointment at the Tax Agency (Skatteverket, n.d.). This card will be your form of identification in Sweden. You'll need it when you go to doctor's appointments, pick up packages from the post office or open a bank account. Speaking of opening a bank account. How do you do that?

Opening a Swedish bank account

Once you have your personal ID number and your Swedish ID card, you can open a bank account in Sweden. Opening an account is usually a relatively straightforward process. You go to the bank, provide your documents, and fill out some paperwork. You'll generally receive a debit card in the mail within a few weeks.

The documents the bank may wish to see vary from bank to bank and depending on which service you are interested in. However, some things you might want to bring with you are (Expat Focus, n.d.):

- Your Swedish ID-card
- Your *personnummer* (Swedish ID number)
- Your passport
- Your residence permit

- Your employment details (e.g., an employment contract or evidence of your income)

As for which bank to choose, there are many options. Do your research based on what services and factors appeal to you, but we also recommend going to the bank in person. If you're trying to choose between a few banks, discussing the information face to face will be very helpful. A few of the most commonly used banks in Sweden are:

- SEB (Skandinaviska Enskilda Banken)
- Swedbank
- Nordea Bank
- Handelsbanken

Here are three common types of accounts you might encounter in Sweden:

- *Nuvarande konto*: Current/checking account. This is a standard account that will give you a debit card and online banking. There is usually little to no interest on the funds.
- *Kapitalkonto*: Savings/deposit account.
- *Kreditkort*: Credit card account.

The regular opening hours for banks in Sweden are Monday to Friday from 10am to 4pm. On Thursdays, banks are usually open until 6pm. This means that banks are closed on weekends, and they are also closed on public holidays.

Getting a Bank ID

To make your life in Sweden easier, make sure to also ask your bank for a Bank ID. This is a way to identify yourself electronically. It's issued by banks and will give you access to many services offered by public agencies. A BankID is the go-to way Swedes sign agreements and tax returns. It's how they collect packages from a postal agent or pay securely on the internet, and so much more.

To get a BankID, you need to have a *personnummer* and a bank account with a bank that issues BankID. The following banks are all connected:

- Danske Bank in Sweden
- Handelsbanken
- Ica Banken
- Länsförsäkringar Bank
- Nordea
- SEB
- Skandiabanken
- Sparbanken Syd
- Swedbank
- Ålandsbanken in Sweden

You order your BankID directly from your bank. A BankID is used on your computer, but there is also a much-appreciated mobile version called Mobile BankID, for smartphones and tablets. To use it, you'll have to download the Mobile BankID app, which is available on Google Play and the Appstore. Then, you can log in to your online bank and get an activation code to activate your Mobile BankID.

Once you have a Swedish BankID, you can also get Swish, which we'll discuss more below under the subheading "What's Swish?"

Getting a cellphone plan

After arriving, you'll need a way to stay in touch with friends back home and be reachable in your new country. You likely have a phone with you, but you'll probably need a phone plan.

There are many mobile operators to choose from. We list some of the leading phone companies here:

- Telenor
- Comviq
- Tre
- Halebop
- Hallon
- Vimla

Depending on what you value in a phone plan, every mobile operator has different pros and cons! We recommend that you look up some of the recommended mobile operators and compare their services before making your choice. Each operator will have different offers. Try to decide which factors are essential for you. Here are some questions to have in mind:

- Does the operator offer customer service in English?
- Does the offer include international calls?
- How many GB are included?

When getting a phone plan, you'll come across different types of subscriptions. Two of the most common types of mobile plans are:

- Abonnemang: Contract. This can be a good option if you're staying in Sweden for a longer time. With a contract, you might get good deals, but make sure to always read the terms and conditions to be aware of costs and fees.
- Kontantkort: Prepaid. You can also use a prepaid plan, which is flexible and can be a good option if you stay in Sweden for a shorter time.

While we're on the subject of phones, we'd like to mention country calling codes international direct dial (IDD). If you have never lived abroad before, you might not have needed to use a country code when placing calls before. Each country has a country code, and if you want to call home from Sweden, you'll need to add the country code to the number.

Most countries have two-digit codes. The UK has 44, France has 33, and Sweden has 46. The US is an exception, with just 1 as its country code. Some smaller countries have country codes that are three digits.

Apart from this, you'll also have to use something called an IDD. This is an international phone code or call prefix you add to an international number. For the majority of the world, the IDD is 011 or 00. For example, if you are in the

US or Canada, you will use 011, whereas you will use 00 if you're in a country within the European Union. It is often written as a +, which can often be used to replace the IDD.

In summary, to make an international call, you'll have to write the IDD, the country code, and then the phone number. If the phone number starts with a 0, you leave this 0 out. As an example, if you want to call the Swedish phone number 09999 99999, you will call one of the following:

- 011 46 9999 99999
- 00 46 9999 99999
- +46 9999 99999

Summary

You're finally in Sweden! What are the things you'll have to do after you've arrived? Let's take everything one step at a time.

One of the first things we recommend you to do is book an appointment at Migrationsverket (the Swedish Migration Agency) to get your residence permit. That is if you don't already have your permit.

Another vital step is to register with Skatteverket (the Swedish Tax Agency). When you've registered, you'll receive your *personnummer*. This is your personal identification number or Swedish ID number. Your legal identity in Sweden hinges on this number. You'll also have to book an appointment at Skatteverket to get a Swedish ID card.

You can now open a Swedish bank account. The process is pretty straightforward. You go to the bank, provide your documents, and fill out some paperwork. You'll generally receive a debit card in the mail within a few weeks.

Make sure to also ask your bank for a BankID, which will allow you to identify yourself electronically. A BankID is very valuable, as it will give you access to many public services.

Of course, you might also need a cell phone plan. We recommend that you look up some of the recommended mobile operators and compare their services before making your final choice.

Acclimatizing to life in Sweden

There will likely be a few things about life in Sweden you'll need time to acclimatize to. Perhaps it's the lack of cash, the price of plastic bags, or how to buy alcohol in Sweden. We'll attempt to explain some of these aspects of Swedish life so that you'll hopefully get used to them as soon as possible!

A cash-free society

One characteristic of Swedish life you'll notice pretty quickly is the lack of cash. While many countries might have stores that are "Cash only", many places in Sweden are "Cash-free" or "Card only". If you're not accustomed to making payments electronically, it's definitely something you'll have to grow accustomed to. Fast.

Is Sweden really a cash-free society? That depends on when you're reading this book. Sweden has been working towards the goal of getting rid of cash for a while. And the country is paving its way to becoming the first cashless society by March 24, 2023 (Fourtané, 2020). After that date, cash is no longer meant to be accepted. That's right, Swedish coins and banknotes will soon belong in museum collections rather than wallets.

What's Swish?

Speaking of Sweden's lack of cash, it's impossible not to also mention Swish. Except for using cards, mobile payment services are also becoming a part of the culture. Swish is the foremost example and deserves a subheading of its own.

Swish is a simple app that allows you to make instant money transfers to other accounts. You download Swish onto your smartphone and connect your phone number with your Swedish bank account. You can then quickly pay for something or send money to a friend in a matter of seconds. All you need is their phone number. You approve payments swiftly and safely with a mobile BankID. The app has become so widespread in Sweden that the verb *swisha* (to swish) has become part of the everyday language (Sweden.se, 2021e).

Recycle and reuse

If you've done your research, you'll know that Swedes feel strongly about recycling and the environment. Sweden aims for zero waste. To accomplish that, every person living in Sweden has to reevaluate their behavior. That means you too. Whether you want to or not, you will be affected by the environmentally-conscious culture of Sweden.

99% of Sweden's locally produced waste is recycled, with only 1% going to landfills (Daily Scandinavian, 2019). Separating cartons and packages for recycling when throwing away garbage is already second nature to many Swedes. There're also many companies in Sweden primarily focused on helping people make better choices in their daily habits. For example, the start-up *Beteendelabbet* (Swedish for "the behavior laboratory") works on finding solutions for sustainable living and motivating people to reuse and recycle (Sweden.se, 2021f).

For example, you might notice that plastic bags in grocery stores feel pricey. Sweden has had a levy on plastic bags since 2020. This means that you'll often pay 6 or 7 SEK per plastic bag, which is around 0,76 USD or 0,64 EUR. People are encouraged to reuse their plastic bags or bring their own bags to carry groceries. It will undoubtedly save you a bit of money to join that habit.

Sweden's deposit system for recycling cans and bottles is another system ingrained into the Swedish mentality. It's called *pantsystemet*, often mentioned as "the pant system" in English, but rest assured that pants are not involved. The Swedish word *pant* simply means deposit. When Swedes buy products in bottles or cans, for example, a beer bottle or a soda can, they pay a deposit. Swedes are encouraged to recycle cans and bottles at the recycling machine stations outside of grocery stores instead of throwing them away. When they do so, the deposit they paid is returned to them. This refund is a part of the incentive of this system. In Sweden, it's not uncommon to come across the sight of a slightly hung-over Swede with bags full of empty bottles left over after a party. Yes, they are heading to the grocery store to get that deposit refund.

This recycling system has been giving people back their money since 1984. Swedes recycle 1,8 billion cans and bottles each year that would otherwise be thrown away. Most people don't think twice about it. The act of recycling cans and bottles even has its own verb, *panta*.

The alcohol monopoly

Another thing you might need to get used to is how to buy alcohol in Sweden. If you go to a restaurant or a bar, you can buy a drink there. However, if you wish to buy more potent alcohol from a store, you'll soon realize the options are minimal. In fact, you only have one choice.

That option is Systembolaget. Systembolaget is Swedish for "the system company", and it's a state-owned and nationwide chain of stores. These stores are the only stores allowed to sell strong alcoholic drinks in Sweden (Routes North, 2016). This is usually something that non-Swedish people will have to get used to.

Why does Systembolaget exist? The primary purpose is to ensure that alcohol is sold responsibly and to minimize alcohol-related problems. According to studies, most Swedes (over 70%) support Systembolaget's monopoly (Systembolaget, 2019).

The opening hours are another thing to keep in mind. Systembolaget closes in the early afternoon on Saturdays and is always closed on Sundays. That means that if you're having a party on Sunday evening, you better remember to buy alcohol earlier during the week.

Speaking of opening hours, what are the regular opening hours in Sweden? Opening hours can vary significantly from store to store and city to city. But it's good to be aware that banks are closed on weekends. You will, however, find stores, post offices, and pharmacies open on weekends, even though they might close a bit earlier than on weekdays. Of course, stores might have different opening hours on certain public holidays. Make sure to check out our list of public holidays in our section "Useful links and resources".

If you want to pick up some beer or other alcoholic beverages from a supermarket or convenience store, you can. BUT they are forbidden from selling alcoholic drinks that exceed 3,5% in alcoholic strength (Routes North, 2016). So, the beer or cider you might find will either be alcohol-free, or have a strength at or below 3,5%.

What about the age limit? You can buy alcohol at restaurants and bars when you are 18. However, the age limit for buying alcohol at Systembolaget is 20. Be prepared to show an ID when you buy alcohol at Systembolaget. The staff can deny your purchase if you are under 20 or look young and don't have an ID to confirm your age. They can also deny your purchase if you have clearly had too much to drink when you try to make the purchase or if they suspect that you are buying alcohol for minors.

Drink your tap water

The norm for drinking water in Sweden is drinking tap water! The tap water in Sweden is clean and fresh (Routes North, 2021g). The water you can buy in convenience stores is usually fairly pricey, so you'll definitely save money by bringing a bottle with you. And not buying bottled water is not only good for your wallet, but for the environment too.

Cold and dark winters

Sweden's winters are dark and cold. Most people expect the cold and will come prepared with warm clothes. But some are less prepared for the darkness. As winter approaches, the days get shorter and shorter, and the chances of getting some sunlight decrease significantly.

For many people, the lack of sunlight can be a shock. It can also lead to a lack of vitamin D, making you feel tired or sometimes even depressed (Sveriges Radio, 2015). Some choose to take vitamin D supplements to battle the lack of sun.

Reserved people

Speaking of Swedish winters, many might also find Swedes to be rather cold at first. Compared to many other cultures, Swedish people are often regarded as quite reserved and hard to make friends with. Many Swedes stick to spending time with a few close friends that they feel completely comfortable with. Stockholmers especially have a rumor of not being a particularly friendly bunch. There are naturally many exceptions, and we certainly hope you'll find some warm, bubbly Swedes to talk to when you arrive.

This aspect of the Swedish personality is, however, something to be aware of. It can take time before Swedes warm up to you and feel comfortable talking about more profound subjects. When you have just met somebody, topics such as their personal background or income are probably best avoided. On the bus, Swedes will do their best to sit as far away from strangers as possible. Unless you want a displeased Swede, don't sit next to them on public transport if other seats are available.

Is there a solution? One suggestion is to find common interests. Perhaps attend activities surrounding sports teams, or maybe a book club? Bars are always a good option, as a drink or two might help the shy Swedes to get chattier.

Summary

You'll probably need time to acclimatize to certain aspects of life in Sweden. Like what?

One characteristic of Swedish life you'll notice pretty quickly is the lack of cash. Be prepared to use your card or phone to pay for everything. The most popular mobile payments service in Sweden is Swish, which you will definitely benefit from downloading.

Swedes also feel strongly about recycling, and you will be expected to be more environmentally conscious while living there. If nothing else, you'll be paying a higher price for plastic bags. Sweden's deposit system for recycling cans and bottles is another system ingrained into the Swedish mentality. It even has its own Swedish verb, *panta*.

Another thing that can take getting used to is the Swedish alcohol monopoly. That's right, if you want to buy a strong alcoholic drink from a store, you only have one option: Systembolaget. This is a state-owned and nationwide chain of stores. Other stores or supermarkets are only allowed to sell alcoholic drinks with a maximum of 3,5% in alcoholic strength. Speaking of drinking, you might also have to get used to drinking from the tap. Yup, drinking clean and fresh tap water is the norm in Sweden.

Most people are prepared for the Swedish winters to be cold, but they are also dark. Sorry about that. Prepare mentally for the lack of sun. Speaking of the freezing temperatures, many also find Swedes to be somewhat reserved and cold at first. They may need some time to warm up to new people, so be patient.

Integrating into Swedish society

To get as much out of your Swedish experience, you won't just want to acclimatize to life in Sweden. You'll also want to integrate into Swedish society. It's not necessarily an easy task. We're here to give you some tips to keep in mind.

Customs, culture, and characteristics

If you're already working on your Swedish language skills, well done! But to fully integrate into Swedish society, you will also need to understand Swedish behavior. Like all countries, Sweden has its unique customs, and Swedes have characteristics that make them, well, Swedish. Let's talk about some quirks you might want to be aware of.

A small disclaimer: All Swedes are individuals who have their own ideas and habits. You might have a Swedish friend who doesn't agree with the following characteristics at all. We provide the following thoughts to help you have a general idea of some common characteristics.

Informality

First of all, you might be aware of how informal Swedes can be with names. In many places around the world, you will address people with titles such as Mr. and Mrs. or by their job titles. In Sweden, expect people to call you by your first name. And for them to expect you to call them by their first name. This goes for basically everyone, including your university professor, your boss, and your doctor. It's not Mr. Pettersson, it's Johan. It's not Doctor Lind, it's Hanna. Of course, there might be a few exceptions to this rule. If you come across someone from the Swedish royal family or find yourself in a courtroom, you might want to stick to the titles.

Punctuality

So, Swedes are casual with names, but they're a bit stricter when it comes to being on time. If you're invited to someone's house for dinner, you are generally expected to arrive on time. Not early. Not late. On time. Swedes value punctuality, so if you wish to please, make a note to show up on time for interviews, meetings, appointments, and other events. Oh, and bad weather is no excuse. Some countries cancel school or work on snow days, but this is not the case in Sweden. So, don't think you can stay home from work just because it's snowing outside.

No shoes indoors!

Speaking of showing up to a someone's home for dinner, don't forget to take off your shoes! Yes, really. In many countries, people wear shoes in their private residences and naturally expect guests to do the same. It might even seem rude to ask someone to take off their shoes before entering a house in some cultures. In Sweden, however, the opposite is true. Most Swedes don't wear shoes in their homes and will expect you to take them off before entering as well. Leave those boots at the entrance!

No bragging

Another thing to avoid is bragging. Remember *Jantelagen*? *Jantelagen* or The Law of Jante is a mentality in Nordic countries with the general idea being that "You are not better than anyone else". Many Swedes who follow this rule will avoid bragging or making themselves out to be more than they are. It goes hand in hand with the concept of *lagom*, where nothing, not even people, should be too little or too much, but just enough. This means that you might come across a few frowns if you start bragging about your success or possessions.

Taboo conversational topics

Bragging is one of the big taboos in Sweden. Perhaps related to this is the dislike of using a lot of superlatives when you speak. Compared to other countries, Swedes are more often against stretching the truth. We can't mention all the social taboos to avoid. Still, Swedish people, in general, try to shy away from discussions related to religion and politics. If you wish to please the people around you, so will you. It's also good to be aware that jokes about sexist or racist stereotypes will probably not gain you a lot of friends. Oh, and if there is only one piece of cake left on the plate, don't take it. Just trust us.

Keep up to date on current affairs

Most Swedes try to stay on top of world events, and while you're in Sweden, it doesn't hurt to keep up to date on Swedish news. Radio Sweden (Sveriges Radio) is the national radio, and they have some news in other languages. They also have a page for news in "Simple Swedish" for newcomers to Sweden. A few other popular online news options include

Aftonbladet and SVT news. One popular Swedish general news website in English is The Local.

Summary

When it comes to the customs, culture, and characteristics of Swedes, there are some quirks you might want to be aware of. First of all, Swedes can be very informal with names. Swedes will expect you to call them by their first name. That includes your boss.

On the other hand, Swedes are stricter when it comes to time. Be punctual if you want to please. And bad weather is no excuse. Staying home because it's a "snow day" is not a thing in Sweden.

When you're (punctually) arriving to someone's home in Sweden, don't forget to take off your shoes! Yes, really. Most Swedes don't wear shoes in their homes, and it would be quite a shock if you did not comply.

What about taboos in Sweden? To sum up a few, don't brag, don't talk about politics or religion, and don't grab the last piece of cake.

If you want to find conversation topics, you might want to stay on top of world events and Swedish news. Be sure to check out some Swedish news options to keep up to date.

Learning Swedish

For full integration into Swedish society, learning Swedish is instrumental. Swedes are commonly viewed as having an impressive level of English. And most people you meet on the street will indeed be able to communicate with you in English. However, as with most countries, the language is a part of the culture and the mindset of the people.

Unfortunately, something that makes learning Swedish more difficult is the point we just mentioned. Many Swedes have a high English proficiency, so they will likely just switch to speaking English when communicating with you. This means fewer opportunities for you to practice. So, if you wish to practice your Swedish, you might have to insist that your Swedish friend speaks Swedish with you.

Where to start? If you're going to Sweden as a university student, you can see if your school offers Swedish courses for international students. There are also language cafés, where you can practice Swedish in a more informal setting. What better way to learn Swedish than over a *fika*? You can usually find a large number of language cafés around universities.

Websites and apps

Today there are more and more options to learn Swedish online through various apps and websites. Some options include the websites SwedishPod101.com, Babbel, and Italki, and the apps Learning Swedish and Duolingo. Let's look into some of these options.

SwedishPod101.com

SwedishPod101.com is a website that provides short audio and video lessons. You can also boost your learning with vocabulary lists, slideshows, and flashcards. With a Premium PLUS subscription, you can learn 1-on-1 with your own online Swedish teacher. The website has four subscription levels: Free, Basic, Premium, and Premium PLUS.

Subscription prices range from 8 USD/month to 47 USD/month.

Babbel

With Babbel, you can take quick lessons on your computer or on a mobile device. It's an excellent resource for foundational Swedish, using a variety of exercises.

The price for personal plans range between 6,95 and 12,95 USD/month.

Italki

On Italki, you can choose a teacher or tutor to work with you 1-on-1. If you know that you're the kind of learner that needs a teacher to communicate with, that's a big plus.

Prices range from 4 USD/hour with an average of 10 USD/hour, so you'll be able to choose an hourly rate that works for you.

Learning Swedish

Learning Swedish is an app created by the Swedish Institute and partners. It has videos, exercises, flashcards, and level tests.

The basic course is free, but the teacher-led courses are quite pricey, starting at 350 USD.

Duolingo

Duolingo is an app that teaches students Swedish and other languages through a variety of engaging exercises. Lessons get progressively harder so that you can see your improvement. Using the app is free, but you can also sign up for Duolingo Plus for 6,99 USD/month.

Swedish for immigrants

If you already have your personal ID number (*personnummer*), you will also be happy to know about SFI. SFI stands for *Svenska för invandrare* (Swedish for Immigrants). It's a free Swedish language program that is open to adult immigrants.

SFI is a beginner's course and provides basic knowledge of the Swedish language and society. The goal is to help you communicate in both written and oral forms. You can apply to SFI by contacting the private SFI provider in your municipality or the adult education department of your city.

Reactions to SFI vary. Some are pretty happy with it, whereas others have complaints. This is perhaps not surprising, as the quality of the teaching can vary between SFI schools. The learning approach has also been criticized by some. Some individuals in the class will likely find the tempo too slow, while other classmates will find it too fast. The decision is yours, but we say, what's the harm in giving it a try? After all, it's free, and if nothing else, it'll give you a learning structure, a teacher, and classmates to practice with.

Summary

Integrating into Swedish society is not an easy task. An instrumental first step is learning the language. Many Swedes have a high English proficiency, so they might be able to communicate with you just fine. But the language is still an essential part of the culture and the mindset of Swedes. So, try to insist that your Swedish friends speak Swedish with you!

If you're going to Sweden as a university student, see if your school offers Swedish courses for international students. There are also language cafés, where you can practice Swedish in a more informal setting.

There are many websites and apps to try out, including SwedishPod101.com, Babbel, Italki, Learning Swedish, and Duolingo. Make sure to compare these different tools to find the best option for you! You also have SFI, which stands for Svenska för invandrare (Swedish for Immigrants). It's a free Swedish language program for adult immigrants.

You're on your way to Sweden!

We truly hope you've enjoyed the ride! We've tried to guide you through the ups and downs involved with moving to Sweden through this book. Visa, immigration, acclimatizing to a new country – it can be an overwhelming process. Hopefully, this book has been a good friend to you on the journey.

Remember to hang onto the section "Useful links and resources" at the back of the book. You never know when a link or a number might come in handy. We'd love it if you wrote a review about the book if you appreciated it and found it helpful. We wish you the best with all your efforts. Welcome to Sweden!

Useful links and resources

Now, we know having the entire process of moving to Sweden ahead of you can seem overwhelming. The key is to take everything one step at a time. Here, we list useful numbers, websites and other resources that will be of help as you go on this journey.

Useful numbers

- Emergencies (police, ambulance, and fire department): 112
- Medical advice: 1177
- Police for non-emergency incidents: 11 414
- Information about non-emergency accidents and emergencies: 113 13

Useful links

Studying in Sweden

University Admissions (Applying for University): https://www.universityadmissions.se/intl/start

Study in Sweden: https://studyinsweden.se/

Erasmus Program: https://ec.europa.eu/programmes/erasmus-plus/node_en

Nordplus Program: https://www.nordplusonline.org/

Linnaeus-Palme Program: https://en.utbyten.se/our-programmes/linnaeus-palme/

Visa information

Migrationsverket (Swedish Migration Agency): http://www.migrationsverket.se/English/Private-individuals.html

Sweden Abroad (Find your Embassy!): http://www.swedenabroad.com/

Authorities in Sweden

Skatteverket (Swedish Tax Agency): https://skatteverket.se/servicelankar/otherlanguages/inenglish.4.12815e4f14a62bc048f4edc.html

Learning Swedish

SFI/Svenska För Invandrare (Swedish for Immigrants): https://vuxenutbildning.stockholm/sfi/swedish-for-immigrants/

SwedishPod101.com (website): https://www.swedishpod101.com/

Babbel (website): https://www.babbel.com/course-description/learn-swedish-online

Italki (website): https://www.italki.com/teachers/swedish

Learning Swedish (app):
https://apps.apple.com/us/app/learning-swedish-official/id1301180873?l=sv&ls=1

Duolingo (app):
https://www.duolingo.com/course/sv/en/Learn-Swedish

Volunteering

European Solidarity Corps:
https://europa.eu/youth/solidarity/

Job searching

Arbetsförmedlingen (Swedish Public Employment Service):
https://arbetsformedlingen.se/other-languages/english-engelska

Arbetsförmedlingen: Platsbanken:
https://arbetsformedlingen.se/platsbanken/

The Local: https://www.thelocal.se/jobs/

Swedish Jobs: https://swedish.jobs/

Neuvoo: https://se.neuvoo.com/en

Websites for property listings

Hemnet: https://www.hemnet.se/

Boneo: https://www.boneo.se/

Bovision: https://bovision.se/

Booli: https://www.booli.se/

Swedish news

Sveriges Radio (Radio Sweden): https://sverigesradio.se/radioswedenpalattsvenska

Aftonbladet: https://www.aftonbladet.se/

SVT nyheter (SVT news): https://www.svt.se/

The Local: https://www.thelocal.se/

More information about Sweden

Sweden.se: https://sweden.se/

Visit Sweden: https://visitsweden.com/

The Newbie Guide to Sweden: https://www.thenewbieguide.se/

The Local: https://www.thelocal.se/

Naturvårdsverket (Information about *Allemansrätten*): https://www.naturvardsverket.se/om-oss/publikationer/8500/right-of-public-access--a-unique-opportunity/

Public Holidays

Here are some public holidays in Sweden, when most people will be off work, and you might find that shops and stores have different opening times. Besides these holidays, there are also days such as Julafton (Christmas Eve) on the 24th of December where very few people will be working, even though it's not officially a bank holiday.

- Nyårsdagen (New Year's Day): January 1st
- Trettondagen (Epiphany): January 6th
- Långfredagen (Good Friday): The date changes yearly, but is the Friday closest to Easter
- Påskdagen (Easter Sunday): April 4th in 2021
- Annandag påsk (Easter Monday): April 5th in 2021
- Första maj (Labour Day): May 1st
- Kristi Himmelsfärds Dag (Ascension Day): May 13th in 2021
- Nationaldagen (National Day): June 6th
- Juldagen (Christmas Day): December 25th
- Annandagen (Boxing Day): December 26th

References

Arbetsförmedlingen. (n.d.). *Do you want to work in Sweden?* https://arbetsformedlingen.se/other-languages/english-engelska/do-you-want-to-work-in-sweden

British Expat Guide. (2016, October 28). *Immigrating To Sweden: The 5 Best Cities to Live and Work.* https://britishexpatguide.co.uk/moving-to-sweden-the-best-cities-to-live-and-work/

Climates to Travel. (n.d.). *Climate – Sweden.* https://www.climatestotravel.com/climate/sweden

Daily Scandinavian. (2019, October 21). *Exporting Trash to Stockholm.* https://www.dailyscandinavian.com/exporting-trash-to-stockholm/

Educations.com. (2021a, February 8). *TUITION FEES & STUDY COSTS IN SWEDEN.* https://www.educations.com/study-guides/europe/study-in-sweden/tuition-fees-6110

Educations.com. (2021b, February 8). *ENTRY REQUIREMENTS FOR SWEDISH UNIVERSITIES.* https://www.educations.com/study-guides/europe/study-in-sweden/requirements-11344

European Solidarity Corps. (n.d.-a). *Frequently Asked Questions.* European Union. https://europa.eu/youth/solidarity/faq_en

European Solidarity Corps. (n.d.-b). *Volunteering.* European Union.

https://europa.eu/youth/solidarity/youngpeople/volunteering_en

European Solidarity Corps. (n.d.-c). *Traineeships & jobs.* European Union. https://europa.eu/youth/solidarity/youngpeople/traineeships-jobs_en

Expat Focus. (n.d.). *How to Move to Sweden.* https://www.expatfocus.com/sweden/moving/how-to-move-to-sweden/

Experts for Expats. (2017, October 9). *Essential information for taking your pet abroad.* https://www.expertsforexpats.com/relocation/taking-your-pet-abroad/

Experts for Expats. (2021, July 13). *Moving Abroad Checklist.* https://www.expertsforexpats.com/relocation/moving-abroad-checklist/

Fourtané, S. (2020, December 24). *Sweden: How to Live in the World's First Cashless Society.* Interesting Engineering. https://interestingengineering.com/sweden-how-to-live-in-the-worlds-first-cashless-society

Go Overseas. (n.d.-a). *Swedish Language Schools in Sweden.* https://www.gooverseas.com/language-schools/swedish

Go Overseas. (n.d.-b). *Volunteer in Sweden.* https://www.gooverseas.com/volunteer-abroad/sweden

Government Offices of Sweden. (2020, August 19). *List of foreign citizens who require Visa for entry into Sweden.* https://www.government.se/government-policy/migration-

and-asylum/list-of-foreign-citizens-who-require-visa-for-entry-into-sweden/

InterNations GO! (2019, October 14). *A Comprehensive Guide on Relocating to Sweden.* https://www.internations.org/go/moving-to-sweden

InterNations GO! (2020a, August 12). *Everything You Need to Know About Finding a New Home in Sweden.* https://www.internations.org/go/moving-tosweden/housing

InterNations GO! (2020b, March 23). *All You Need to Know About Relocating Your Household Goods and Pets.* https://www.internations.org/go/moving-sweden/relocating

Justine. (2017, January 6). 5 things to pack when you move to Sweden. *Study in Sweden.* https://studyinsweden.se/blogs/2017/01/06/pack-move-sweden/

LivingCost.org. (n.d.). *Cost of Living in Sweden.* https://livingcost.org/cost/sweden

The Local. (2020, August 27). *What extra costs should you budget for when you buy a house in Sweden.* https://www.thelocal.se/20200827/what-extra-costs-should-you-budget-for-when-you-buy-a-house-in-sweden/

Lund University. (2021, March 24). *Study Abroad programmes.* https://www.lunduniversity.lu.se/admissions/exchange-and-study-abroad/study-abroad-programmes

Lund University. (n.d.). *Study Abroad: Swedish as a Foreign Language - Levels 1-4.* https://www.lunduniversity.lu.se/lubas/i-uoh-lu-SFSH11

Lungu, M. (2021, August 24). *How to Get a Student Visa for Sweden*. Mastersportal.
https://www.mastersportal.com/articles/1603/how-to-get-a-student-visa-for-sweden.html

MediCarrera. (n.d.). *LIVING & WORKING IN SWEDEN*.
https://medicarrera.com/living-working-sweden/

Migrationsverket. (2021a, September 2). *Residence permit for studies in higher education*.
https://www.migrationsverket.se/English/Private-individuals/Studying-and-researching-in-Sweden/Higher-education/Residence-permit-for-higher-education.html

Migrationsverket. (2021b, September 8). *Working holiday visa for young people*.
https://www.migrationsverket.se/English/Private-individuals/Working-in-Sweden/Employed/Special-rules-for-certain-occupations-and-citizens-of-certain-countries/Working-holiday-visa-for-young-people.html

Migrationsverket. (2021c, September 8). *ICT permits*.
https://www.migrationsverket.se/English/Private-individuals/Working-in-Sweden/Employed/Special-rules-for-certain-occupations-and-citizens-of-certain-countries/ICT-permit.html

Migrationsverket. (2021d, June 30). *Work, study or live in Sweden for EU/ EEA citizens*.
https://www.migrationsverket.se/English/Private-individuals/EU-citizens-and-long-term-residents/Work-study-or-live-in-Sweden-for-EU-citizens.html

Migrationsverket. (2021e, September 8). *How to apply for a work permit*. https://www.migrationsverket.se/English/Private-individuals/Working-in-Sweden/Employed/How-to-apply.html

Migrationsverket. (2021f, July 30). *Special rules for certain occupations and citizens of certain countries.* https://www.migrationsverket.se/English/Private-individuals/Working-in-Sweden/Employed/Special-rules-for-certain-occupations-and-citizens-of-certaincountries.html

Migrationsverket. (2021g, June 10). *When you are employing someone from a country outside the EU.* https://www.migrationsverket.se/English/Other-operators/Employers/Employing-people-from-non-EU-countries-/When-you-are-employing-someone.html

Migrationsverket. (2021h, September 8). *Work permits for au pairs.* https://www.migrationsverket.se/English/Private-individuals/Working-in-Sweden/Employed/Special-rules-for-certain-occupations-and-citizens-of-certain-countries/Au-pair.html

Migrationsverket. (2021i, September 8). *Visit Sweden for less than 90 days – apply for a visa.* https://www.migrationsverket.se/English/Private-individuals/Visiting-Sweden/Visit-Sweden-for-less-than-90-days---apply-for-a-visa.html

Migrationsverket. (2021j, September 8). *Visit Sweden for more than 90 days.* https://www.migrationsverket.se/English/Private-individuals/Visiting-Sweden/Visit-Sweden-for-more-than-90-days.html

Migrationsverket. (2021k, September 8). *Residence permit for volunteers.* https://www.migrationsverket.se/English/Private-individuals/Working-in-Sweden/Employed/Special-rules-for-certain-occupations-and-citizens-of-certain-countries/Volunteer.html

Migrationsverket. (2021l, March 17). *Volunteering.* https://www.migrationsverket.se/English/Other-operators/Employers/Special-rules-for-certain-occupations-and-citizens-of-certain-countries/Volunteer.html

Migrationsverket. (2021m, September 8). *Traineeship through international exchange.* https://www.migrationsverket.se/English/Private-individuals/Working-in-Sweden/Employed/Special-rules-for-certain-occupations-and-citizens-of-certain-countries/Trainee---international-exchange.html

Migrationsverket. (2021n, September 8). *Internship in connection with higher education.* https://www.migrationsverket.se/English/Private-individuals/Working-in-Sweden/Employed/Special-rules-for-certain-occupations-and-citizens-of-certain-countries/Trainee---higher-education.html

Migrationsverket. (2021o, July 28). *Residence permit to move to a spouse, registered partner or cohabiting partner in Sweden.* https://www.migrationsverket.se/English/Private-individuals/Moving-to-someone-in-Sweden/Spouse-registered-partner-or-cohabiting-partner.html

Migrationsverket. (2021p, August 24). *For close relatives of someone applying for a residence permit to live with you in Sweden.* https://www.migrationsverket.se/English/Private-individuals/Moving-to-someone-in-Sweden/Spouse-registered-partner-or-cohabiting-partner/For-the-relative-in-Sweden.html

Migrationsverket. (2021q, August 30). *Make an online application.* https://www.migrationsverket.se/English/Private-individuals/Moving-to-someone-in-Sweden/Make-an-online-application.html

Migrationsverket. (2021r, June 29). *Changed requirements for permanent residence permits for anyone applying for a residence permit on the basis of a family tie to some-body in Sweden.* https://www.migrationsverket.se/English/Private-individuals/Moving-to-someone-in-Sweden/Nyhetsarkiv/2021-06-29-Changed-requirements-for-permanent-residence-permits-for-anyone-applying-for-a-residence-permit-on-the-basis-of-a-family-tie-to-somebody-in-Sweden.html

Migrationsverket. (2021s, June 15). *Instructions for online application for applicants who are married or cohabiting with someone in Sweden.* https://www.migrationsverket.se/English/Private-individuals/Moving-to-someone-in-Sweden/Spouse-registered-partner-or-cohabiting-partner/Instructions-for-online-application.html

Migrationsverket. (2021t, July 28). *After a decision has been made on a residence permit for work in Sweden.* https://www.migrationsverket.se/English/Private-individuals/Working-in-Sweden/Employed/After-the-decision-has-been-made.html

Nomad Guide. (2021, April 6). *The Best Places to Live in Sweden & the Cheapest Cities.* https://nomadguide.eu/cheapest-places-to-live-in-sweden/

Pop, A. (2021, August 19). *Tuition Fees and International Scholarships in Sweden.* Mastersportal.

https://www.mastersportal.com/articles/356/tuition-fees-and-international-scholarships-in-sweden.html

Qvist H.-P.Y., Folkestad B., Fridberg T., Lundåsen S.W. (2019) Trends in Volunteering in Scandinavia. In: Henriksen L., Strømsnes K., Svedberg L. (eds) *Civic Engagement in Scandinavia. Nonprofit and Civil Society Studies (An International Multidisciplinary Series)*. Springer, Cham. https://doi.org/10.1007/978-3-319-98717-0_3

Routes North. (n.d.-a). *IS AIRBNB LEGAL IN SWEDEN?* https://www.routesnorth.com/planning-trip-sweden/frequently-asked-questions/is-airbnb-legal-in-sweden/

Routes North. (n.d.-b). *CAN I STILL PAY WITH CASH IN SWEDEN?* https://www.routesnorth.com/planning-trip-sweden/frequently-asked-questions/can-pay-cash-sweden/

Routes North. (2016, August 14). *SURVIVING SWEDEN'S ALCOHOL MONOPOLY.* https://www.routesnorth.com/planning-your-trip/surviving-swedens-alcohol-monopoly/

Sager, A.-K. (2021, March 11). 14 Best Apps to Learn Swedish Right Now [2021]. *Hey Explorer.* https://heyexplorer.com/apps-to-learn-swedish/

Skatteverket. (n.d.). *ID card.* https://www.skatteverket.se/servicelankar/otherlanguages/inenglish/individualsandemployees/livinginsweden/idcard.4.7be5268414bea064694c420.html

SCB. (2021, March 25). *Invandring till Sverige.* https://www.scb.se/hitta-statistik/sverige-i-siffror/manniskorna-i-sverige/invandring-till-sverige/

Stimac, V. (2020, October 14). The Top 7 Cities for Studying Abroad in Sweden. *Go Overseas.* https://www.gooverseas.com/blog/top-cities-study-abroad-sweden

Study in Sweden. (n.d.-a). *The Swedish Way.* https://studyinsweden.se/moving-to-sweden/the-swedish-way/

Study in Sweden. (n.d.-b). *Accommodation & budget.* https://studyinsweden.se/moving-to-sweden/accommodation-budget/

Study.eu. (n.d.-a). *Study in Sweden.* https://www.study.eu/country/sweden

Study.eu. (n.d.-b). *Study in Uppsala, Sweden.* https://www.study.eu/city/uppsala

Studying in Sweden. (n.d.-a). *Working while Studying.* https://studying-in-sweden.com/working-while-studying/

Studying in Sweden. (n.d.-b). *How to Apply.* https://studying-in-sweden.com/how-to-apply/

Studying in Sweden. (n.d.-c). *Sweden Visas and Immigration.* https://studying-in-sweden.com/visas-and-immigration/

Sveriges Radio. (2015, March 19). *Every other Swede suffers from lack of vitamin D in the winter.* https://sverigesradio.se/artikel/6120407

Sweden.se. (2021a, June 1). *Key facts about Sweden.* https://sweden.se/life/society/key-facts-about-sweden

Sweden.se. (2021b, August 9). *Why work in Sweden?* https://sweden.se/work-business/working-in-sweden/why-work-in-sweden

Sweden.se. (2021c, August 19). *Religion in Sweden.* https://sweden.se/life/society/religion-in-sweden

Sweden.se. (2021d, June 1). *Moving to Sweden in 10 steps.* https://sweden.se/work-business/moving-to-sweden/moving-to-sweden-in-10-steps

Sweden.se. (2021e, June 1). *A cashless society.* https://sweden.se/life/society/a-cashless-society

Sweden.se. (2021f, June 1). *Recycling and beyond.* https://sweden.se/climate/sustainability/recycling-and-beyond

Systembolaget. (2019). *Systembolaget's 2019 Responsibility Report.* https://www.omsystembolaget.se/globalassets/pdf/om-systembolaget/responsibility-report-2019.pdf

University World News. (2020, September 30). *International student numbers up 13% despite COVID-19.* https://www.universityworldnews.com/post.php?story=20200930054856301

Visit Sweden. (2021, August 31). *About the right to access Swedish nature.* https://visitsweden.com/what-to-do/nature-outdoors/nature/sustainable-and-rural-tourism/about-the-right-of-public-access/

Visit Sweden. (2020, November 19). *Skiing in Sweden.* https://visitsweden.com/what-to-do/nature-outdoors/winter-activities/skiing-sweden/

Wise. (2017, November 14). *Getting health insurance in Sweden: A complete guide.* https://wise.com/gb/blog/health-insurance-sweden

Printed in Great Britain
by Amazon